Figuring Sh*t Out

THE GUIDEBOOK FOR LANDING A JOB
WITHIN YOUR FIELD OF STUDY
FRESH OUT OF COLLEGE

by Alexis Thrower

DORRANCE PUBLISHING CO
EST. 1920
PITTSBURGH, PENNSYLVANIA 15238

The contents of this work, including, but not limited to, the accuracy of events, people, and places depicted; opinions expressed; permission to use previously published materials included; and any advice given or actions advocated are solely the responsibility of the author, who assumes all liability for said work and indemnifies the publisher against any claims stemming from publication of the work.

All Rights Reserved
Copyright © 2022 by Alexis Thrower

No part of this book may be reproduced or transmitted, downloaded, distributed, reverse engineered, or stored in or introduced into any information storage and retrieval system, in any form or by any means, including photocopying and recording, whether electronic or mechanical, now known or hereinafter invented without permission in writing from the publisher.

Dorrance Publishing Co
585 Alpha Drive
Pittsburgh, PA 15238
Visit our website at *www.dorrancebookstore.com*

ISBN: 978-1-6366-1237-9
eISBN: 978-1-6366-1824-1

Figuring Sh*t Out

THE GUIDEBOOK FOR LANDING A JOB
WITHIN YOUR FIELD OF STUDY
FRESH OUT OF COLLEGE

This book is dedicated to:

Daeshunn DuPree (Brother)
Maurice Lavell Thrower (Granddad)
Quintin Lee Page (Cousin)
LaKesha Gamble-Thrower (Stepmom)
May you all rest in peace.

Contents

Preface: Who the Hell Am I? ix
Introduction xxv
Understand Your Drive 1
Know Your Purpose and Stay Focused 13
Don't Half-Ass Shit. 23
Reset and Rejuvenate Your Mindset 37
Develop and Maintain Strong Classroom Practices. 41
Internships 45
Networking. 53
Job Search Jumpstart 65
Don't Be a Hater 73
Fast Before You Ask 85

Preface

Who the Hell Am I?

For starters, thank you for taking the time to read my book. I've always been eager, especially when seeking answers to big questions. I followed suit in college, as I was on the hunt to find the best way to land a job within my field of study fresh out of college. While in undergrad, I quickly realized I wasn't alone, as many of my college counterparts were in search of the same answers. This may be your case, which is why you probably selected my book along your path. Out of all the books you could have blindly chosen, with hopes its pages would reveal answers on your road to success, you chose my book. For that, I am beyond grateful.

From motivational books, speakers, and the hundreds of seminars you could have attended on the topic of career advancement and personal development, I am thankful that you have entrusted me with your time. With that responsibility, I hope my story will impact your life and uplift your spirit as you continue your academic journey. This book is also a great addition to your library as a recent graduate. I trust something from my journey will resonate within your soul and add that extra fire to your drive as you navigate life as an adult actively on the job hunt, post-undergrad. Either way, I pray this book finds you at the exact time you need it most.

Before proceeding, please understand this book is by no means my way to save the world. My sole intention isn't to preach at you. If anything, I may cuss at you a little! I am your friend by way of commonalities such as education, young adulthood, goals, and prayer. With these shared experiences, I hope you reflect on my life experiences so you might have a clearer understanding of the next steps you should consider within yours. My prayer over your life is that you become perfectly attuned to the signs that God is placing in your life to hint at what He has ordained specifically for you. I use this book to reach the special demographic of students and recent grads who have freely fantasized about all the things their life can be and all the places they can go after graduating but are introduced to the harsh reality that simply having the degree is not going to cut it.

I knew when writing this book, it was not the time to casually slip into my bubbly naivety, when like you, I was also navigating young adulthood in a world heavily comprised of conflicting and discouraging information. I often heard that if I kept applying myself, I would be okay because, "only the strong survive." On the other hand, I was also met with the notion that no matter what I did to get ahead in life, the rich would only get richer, while the poor would get poorer. This can cause anyone to feel defeated before their journey even truly begins. As you read, I urge you to consider my philosophy of doing away with the hearsay. Be open to how the experiences of others add to your life. Build on successful practices you've witnessed and experienced to consistently strive in your respective academic discipline. Be confident in your approach to go through trial and error to figure shit out and trust that you were called to do whatever God set out for you to do.

I stand firm in my beliefs that we can all learn from someone else's path, no matter the age, race, sex, or any other differentiating identifier. We don't have to perpetuate a cycle of doing what we saw or heard growing up because it's familiar. We all have the power to master astute observation in other's experiences by identifying what worked, and steer clear from things that didn't. By doing so, we nourish ourselves in ways which the lessons we learn from others can be used as fuel to do something different and achieve far better for our own lives. With that, it's going to take more than a daydream and prayer to get that job *within your field* after graduating, but I'm here to help you through it all. This book will give you the space to effectively evaluate your experiences and observe the lives of people around you to better outline your game plan for post-undergraduate success. Needless to say, I am elated to have gone through my journey, as I realize my story wasn't simply mine to live, but my experience to share.

I am often confronted by strangers, family members, and acquaintances alike, who make comments along the lines of me being ever so "put together." I could be feeling like absolute shit, but I'm consistently met with a resounding, "Oh, she's so put together. She's gonna be just fine in life." After this was uttered to me for the umpteenth time, the only thought that came to mind was, *If only they knew the half of it.* Even though every fiber of my being wanted to scream because they had no idea what the hell they were talking about, I always politely said, "Thank you," and exited stage left. I found that with demonstrating this professional exterior every waking moment of my life, it placed me in a dangerous position for one's own health and wellness. I started to recognize a pattern. The more I tried to explain to others that everything that glittered in my life wasn't gold, the more dismissive outsiders looking in became of my life, because to them, I was doing "just fine." I realized the more successful I "appeared" to be to others, my circle of people who would tap into my soul and genuinely ask me how I was doing became minuscule. Such a position left me handling more than anyone can bargain for themselves. Some disconnects started to happen in my relationships. Family and friends didn't always understand the sacrifices associated with going to school. I often felt trapped in my own thoughts, incapable of safely sharing my peaks and valleys in undergrad since I came across my fair share of people who easily dismissed the growing pains of a college student as minor compared to the rest of the world. There wasn't always space for me to healthily fall apart to come back stronger. You too, may have to take a few walks alone. It won't be anything personal, but people who aren't riding the same wavelength as you or haven't lived experiences similar to yours simply will not understand. That place can spark depression, discouragement, and leave you wondering "Why me?" As I grew in my adulthood experience and spiritual walk, I had to rephrase my thinking and say, "Why not me?" As cliché as this sounds, most of our experiences require that we go *through it*, to understand the *why* behind it at a later time. This draws back to one of my initial points as I stated, our experiences aren't just for ourselves, but for us to share and help the next person.

Despite feeling extremely low at times, I made a promise to myself that regardless of my circumstances, I'd be damned if I let anyone shake my public walk of confidence. If I failed at everything else that day, I could count on my "power walk." It goes beyond being a literal walk, as a dope ass black woman handling her business in the sleekest of pumps; it's a walk of confidence that I was boldly taking one step in front of the other to fulfill my God-ordained purpose. So yes, to outsiders I have it together. In reality, I'm merely making the sweetest lemonade possible with sour lemons like everyone else. Men have a walk too. You know what it is, fellas. That walk that's kick-started by putting on your most form-fitting suit and a quick polish of your shoes before stepping out on the scene—the feeling that changes everything! That walk is an extension of your poker face. You may have no idea of your next move but there is an inner confidence that you *will* figure it out.

Women and men alike, I urge you to deeply connect with your confidence and hold on to it. That walk and vote of confidence in your damn self is what you'll need to be successful in whatever you do beyond the classroom. As soon as you decide to respect the authority in which you have the power to command, the grind remains difficult, but your delivery, that sweet delivery, will appear effortless. No matter how chaotic your life may be, no matter how frazzled life can make you, always consider how you want to be perceived, and hone in on your God-specific assignment. Handle your stressful affairs privately, but continue to walk with a sense of purpose, even if you haven't figured out what it is yet. In a world where we are constantly on information overload, take advantage of private, quiet moments and talk to God about what He wants you to do with your life. Stay true to this notion especially as a future or recent grad.

In case you still need a reason to continue reading, to dive right in, the very last day of my last final in undergrad, December 8, 2017, marked the same day that an employer reached out to me via email to be considered for my degree-specific job opportunity. After going through the interview procedure, I was extended a formal offer of employment just one month after finishing undergrad. However, my story doesn't begin or end there. December 8, 2017, may have marked the last day of undergrad, but I honored it as the first day of my post-undergraduate life. During my last two days of college, I received emails and phone calls with offers and interview invitations from across the country. Some of those opportunities included option-to-hire news internships, communication jobs with the government, and more. An outpour of communication from various sources were attracted to me like flies on a sticky trap. Instances like this are almost unheard of for people who have been in the workforce for years, let alone a black chick with nothing but greenery on her ass the day after college. While many statistics reflect overall college retention rates, and an even lesser number for those who end up working in their field, and an even lesser number for those obtaining a job so quickly after finishing school, here I was... a grad with options!

A 2018 report conducted by Burning Glass and the Strada Institute for the Future of Work examined underemployment's long-term effects on the careers of college grads. It found that forty-three percent of recent college grads are underemployed in their first job out of college. From that number, two-thirds remain underemployed after five years. The study notes the choice of a first job can have a resounding impact on future employment. Burning Glass's study defined underemployment by understanding employer preferences based on the education they requested on job postings. This accounted for a bachelor's degree or higher as a college-level job. Although this article covered an assortment of elements associated with landing a job, which also included a thorough breakdown of employment rates of college grads within specific industries, one of the key takeaways from the study was to ultimately reinforce the importance to obtain a bachelor's degree at the minimum.

> When bachelor's degree recipients land an appropriate job after graduation, they end up boosting the chances for higher-paying work in the decades that follow. Early employment matters because young workers are gaining critical, transferrable skills in their initial jobs out of college, says Paul E. Harrington, who runs Drexel University's Center for College Affordability and Productivity (Burning Glass et.al, 2018, p.16).

While doing my research to better understand the "why" behind a college student's inability to obtain a job within their field of study, many sources focused on socioeconomic, geographic location, sex, and age factors. One example of that would be the disparity of African American students in impoverished communities. Most black students are statistically doomed from even going to college, let alone being successful while attending. Many of these studies do not focus on the *behavioral patterns* associated with college attendance, which also contributes to the likelihood of obtaining a job within the field of study. Many college students fail to acknowledge that, placing additional doubt on the significance of higher education. It also doesn't help when students probably meet more people who fail to utilize their degree in comparison to those who do. This was another variable I personally witnessed and coupled with the data. I quickly came to understand why some people felt college was a royal waste of time. Four or more years dedicated to a degree you didn't even use. It's no surprise higher education has grown more and more unattractive to the masses. Despite being an advocate for education, I still had my fair share of issues with the structural components of the education system, which probably lent reason to why I was adamant about maximizing my college resources. I was paying for the shit! I refused to just be another body for the system to continue to build billions in revenue off of just to be met with thousands of dollars in debt, and a fancy piece of paper to acknowledge what the hell I'd been doing for four years.

In 1998, acclaimed rapper Ice Cube wrote and made his directorial debut in the film, *The Player's Club*. It centered around the life of Diamond, played by LisaRaye McCoy, a young mother working her way through college majoring in journalism, and doing so by way of stripping. Although I was only three when this movie was released, I have since watched this film time and time again, as it is a major movie staple within the black community. Throughout Diamond's journey, it becomes her responsibility to look after her troubled cousin, Ebony, played by Monica Calhoun, who also gets into the "demon time" business, but far more recklessly than Diamond. At the end of the movie, Diamond and Ebony realize the nightlife isn't for them. Diamond tells Ebony, "Make that money, girl." Ebony replies, "Don't let the money make you." I make this reference because my view on the college setting reverberates along the same lines. Either I was going to work the educational system for my benefit, or the educational structure was going to work me.

Now before you throw my book in the trash for starting contradictory to the intention of writing this book, keep in mind this wasn't written to place sole blame on the societal structure or the systemic inequities that come with education. While data was plentiful with looking at broader scopes that impact one's ability to fulfill a degree and land (or not land) a job within one's field of study, research about college student *practices* to maximize their experience within the educational space to best support their endeavors post-undergrad was not as abundant. When surveying my college counterparts, the elephant in the room, so to speak, was the disregard that some academic downfall was a direct correlation to student accountability or lack thereof. Scholars and their academic behaviors are also active contributors to these poor statistics. Many students are not maximizing all the opportunities in college that better support their postundergraduate transition. Seeing this play out in real time from my college associates, while committing myself to further exploring options to aid in my job placement after school, breathed life into the idea of writing this book.

As for my story, I attended California State University, Los Angeles, double-majored in communication and television, film, and media studies with an emphasis in journalism. I also wrote this book while pursuing my master's in communication from Johns Hopkins University. My key interest at the time had been to become a news anchor, reporter, and college instructor in communication studies. As I progressed in my graduate program, I became more open to any opportunity that allowed me to thoroughly apply communication practices on a small or large scale. Whether that be in the education, journalistic-, or communications-specific sector, I was open to utilizing my academically cultivated skills to explore other industries I may not have considered initially. The focus was to remain intentional with what I went to school for, while bringing diversity to the respective industry I *could* find myself working in without letting my major-specific skills fall by the wayside. At that time, I was focused on breaking into broadcast news. While landing in the anchor chair fresh out of college was far-fetched, like any business, I understood that I had to "get in where I fit in" and go wherever my first opportunity placed me to achieve that dream. Well, only a month after completing undergrad, I was formally offered a news producer job in Oregon. The beginning stages of this book were actually drafted *en route* to Oregon. Now that you know exactly what happened with my early career from the beginning of this book, as you continue to read, I'll take you on the journey of exactly how I did it.

I hope you will push yourself to consistently brainstorm strategies to further your career and find comfort in knowing you've explored all aspects of your current situation and academic experience to better yourself long term. Chances are, there will always be something more you can do. For my less enthusiastic and procrastinating friends who can only see within the circumference of their present, this is a time to push yourself to think beyond your current conditions.

This is the time to take the necessary steps to manifest lifelong benefits. I urge you to exercise the question of "What more can I do?" within your vocabulary to not only set yourself up for success, but break the habits of procrastination and unpreparedness. We'll touch on the dangers of this later in the book, but for overachievers and underachievers alike, your objective is to find a small sense of accomplishment with what you've done in a day's work to further yourself. Once that's done, you can put the rest in God's hands. For me, I realized, the more I pushed myself, there was a conversion in the question going from "What more can I do?" to "Am I even doing enough?" This book promotes self-reflection and encourages you to ask and answer tough questions about your life. For example, look at your peers. Can you honestly say you are the hardest working person you know? If the answer is a resounding "Yes," then the surrounding elements in your life will validate it. If the answer is "No," then you're not giving yourself a fighting chance. If the people around you aren't working diligently and productively to improve their circumstances, then they are taking up space meant for you to self-improve. It's not too late though to either stay on track or get back on track. I hope this book helps better guide your path.

As you are figuring out your purpose, the premise of this book is to spark self-reflection and evaluate your current situational climate to establish an awareness of what more you can do to land that job within your field fresh out of college. With that, if you are currently in college, take a moment to genuinely evaluate how you would classify yourself based on your academic and behavioral patterns. Examine your skills, your relationship with your professors, and an assortment of other factors that make you, you. This is the time to reflect if you are doing too much. Are you doing enough? Are you setting a generous amount of time aside to study effectively? What would motivate you to get ready to take on new practices now? Take a few moments and jot some thoughts down. Please be honest with yourself. No one has to see this but you.

_____

_____

_____

_____

_____

Figuring Sh*t Out

If you're struggling to answer some of these questions, keep a journal for a few weeks and log your behavioral patterns. This isn't meant to overly criticize yourself or even change up your behaviors. It's simply a reference tool when establishing the significant difference between your perception of yourself and the reality of your life. This documentation forces personal accountability for one's actions. The reality is, your notes won't change when you are reviewing them, so your documentation has no reason to lie to you. For example, if you had one too many drinks on Friday, Saturday, and Sunday, or every weekend of the month, write it down. If you found yourself immensely overwhelmed cramming for that midterm because there is no record of when you set a consistent time to study, write it down. If you smoked a little too much weed and let your entire study day slip, write it down. If something legitimate and completely unexpected happens in life that pulls you away from getting some work done, write it down (this is guaranteed to happen to all of us and will be discussed in a later chapter). For a few weeks, I challenge you to take it a step further. Along with monitoring your day-to-day operations, as you hear people describe you in casual conversation, make a note of those descriptive words. I don't advise you to blatantly ask people, "So hey, what do you think of me?" I guarantee that with putting them on the spot, your findings will be skewed, as human nature aims to please. By doing this, there is a likelihood that most of your feedback will be positively one-sided, or even worse, a flat out lie. The organic information you are truly seeking will come up in a simple conversation. Simply notate what you hear as you continue to do whatever it is you do. It could be something as simple as sitting in the library and a former professor approaches your workstation and says, "You're hardworking, and you're going places." It can be as extreme as listening to a roommate yell, "You're a lazy piece of shit who does nothing but go out!" Simply add their feedback to your notebook.

After you've done some personal reflection, it is time to analyze the data. Examining your recorded entries, see if what others have said about you is consistent with some traits you found within yourself based on your current lifestyle. This will present you with valuable insight that will help better gauge the consistencies and discrepancies of the perception and reality of your life. For example, I studied all the time. If I wasn't at work I was studying, and vice versa. I ran a strict schedule of when I would study. No matter what time I came home every night, I always stayed up until midnight to hit the books. I enjoyed public speaking and had great relationships with my professors that extended beyond the classroom. I hated being unprepared and not having a plan in place. Knowing that about myself was great, but did others view me the same way? After quietly gathering feedback from others, I found that I was often described as hardworking, well-spoken, highly prepared, smart, having a strong delivery and presence. On the flip side of the coin, I was impatient, a constant bundle of nerves, sometimes snappy over small things, and frankly—uptight. I may have rolled my eyes at a few people who made some of these remarks for the sake of not being confrontational, given my own observations of their situation, but I documented the comments, nonetheless. We obviously can't please everyone, and you are more than welcome to agree to disagree, especially if your critic's delivery is piss poor and doesn't come from a place of courtesy and love. This exercise is not meant to spark some back alley brawl. The premise is to hear how others perceive you in order to grow and take the sting out of hearing feedback you should already know about yourself. For example, if you're arguing with someone, the tension of the exchange makes it far harder to listen and understand the feedback, even if there is some truth to their remarks. When feedback comes up casually, we can better receive the content since we aren't immediately on defense. While doing this exercise, remember that you are only collecting data at this time. If you do the exercise correctly, naturally, you will notice that all of your feedback won't be positive. Don't immediately discount the other comments as negative, though. In my case, yes, I may be snappy at times, a little impatient, and have nerves that jump up and down as rapidly as a jackhammer. That doesn't make me an awful human being. These traits make me, me. Fortunately, when doing this exercise, I found that my positive and not-so-positive notes about myself were consistent with the feedback I was hearing from others. This helped me tremendously in defining what I still needed to work on. It also confirmed what I needed to keep doing in college.

After you've done the exercise, you may learn that your findings reveal some discrepancies in how you perceive yourself. Your actions may not be consistent with where you want or need to be. If that's the case, it is okay. If this applies to you, then the next steps are to write out what you envision for yourself. Write down the changes you intend on implementing to ensure that you put action and accountability behind your words, so your present actions create long-term strides in your career.

I think it's safe to say that based on everything I have shared thus far, self-reflection and college and career development is far easier said than done. If you are not prepared to take the necessary steps, I appreciate you being honest with yourself. Thank you for your purchase, but throw my shit in the trash because this book is only for those willing to grind! At least I saved you from further wasting your time with the read. On the flip side, and the equally dangerous side, I know some people will read this book and have themselves thoroughly convinced they are ready to do what needs to be done to set themselves up for a job within their field post-undergrad, despite knowing deep in their gut that they lack the necessary ambition to achieve it. I mark this scenario as equally dangerous, because one of the worst things we can do is work overtime to convince ourselves and those around us that we are doing shit but have absolutely nothing to show for it. This creates a false reality that is extremely difficult to step out of and leaves us racing in a hamster wheel doing the same thing with no new results. Regardless of the side you fall on, consider all I have shared with you thus far and take a moment for some self-reflection. Ask yourself this: Based on your current situation, why do you believe you are ready (or not) to implement new practices that will make your transition into the workforce post-undergrad more efficient?

_____

_____

_____

_____

_____

If you have jotted down some notes that are consistent with you believing in yourself and your ability to actively integrate processes that will be substantial for your career post-undergrad, then kudos to you! This is a great starting point, as you've unlocked the secret to many of life's initiatives, and that's betting on yourself, because no one is going to fight for your passion and dream more than you. If you used this time of reflection to bash yourself, then that's simply the devil at work, and I challenge you to dig deep down and identify one positive attribute about yourself to combat such negativity. If you wrote out reasons why you feel these practices are out of reach, or simply have mixed emotions about your capabilities, then I want you to know that negative self-talk is normal and not a true indicator of your ability to achieve your goals.

If you're anything like me, a person who gets severely caught up in their thoughts, and at a point in my life had a difficult time differentiating God's word, the devil's word, and my self-talk, then let me break it down for you. Some would argue that any negative self-talk is of the devil. I beg to differ, even with my religious and spiritual background, and especially as a stressed out college student. First, let's establish what self-talk is. When reviewing a 2006 article from the *Canadian Journal of Behavioural Science* that explored self-talk and emotional intelligence in university students, it stated, "In past research, self-talk has been studied as a means of enhancing self-awareness, self-regulation, and problem-solving, all of which are interrelated and considered important in the construct of emotional intelligence," (Depape, 2006, p.251). Within my spiritual walk, I recognized that the greatest indicator to determine which voice was speaking to me stemmed from how I felt in the moment. For example, when you're studying for that exam and frivolously make remarks such as, "I'm such an idiot. How'd I miss that?", that's a very superficial comment that doesn't hold significant value on your ability to achieve success on that exam. It may spark some doubt, but it's not a comment that's ruining your day. That's self-talk… negative self-talk. On the spiritual side, at times, it can be hard to tell if it's God or Satan speaking to you, as they both speak directly to your spirit, but manifest completely different physical and mental sensations. It got easier to tell who was speaking to me as I furthered my walk with God. I use a trick to help me decipher the difference. For example, when I hear words spiritually whispered to me, I stop what I am doing and pay attention to what my body is feeling. When I hear whispers in the late-night hours as I'm writing or studying, "You'll never be good enough," or "You should just quit," and "You'll never publish this book," these are words that not only further my frustration, but also spark a muddled disturbance in the pit of my stomach (an extremely unpleasant physical manifestation). I instantly know who and where that information is coming from. However, when God speaks to us, it is always so gentle that if we aren't careful, we often miss what He may be trying to tell us. I know

God is speaking to me without a doubt because His mode of message delivery is one that has a way of tapping into every point of tension in my body and allows my stress to simply melt away. It's such a calming sensation that I immediately recognize I can even breathe a little better than I was a few minutes prior (a positive physical manifestation).

Now that we've established those voices in our heads from a spiritual point of reference, what about negative self-talk? Is that just the devil too? Although we are discouraged to engage in negative self-talk, we wouldn't be people if we didn't do it some of the time. I wouldn't say this is necessarily Satan; it's just human nature. However, there is a difference between negative self-talk and being completely honest with yourself. Although a hard pill to swallow, and a rare one to mix with educational and motivational books, sometimes you have to take a beat and realize you are simply not up for the challenge life is presenting. It's not a matter of talking down to yourself just because, but a necessary reflection if you aren't willing to put in the work to manifest your dreams as reality. It can be uncomfortable when you mentally hold yourself accountable for a lack of intentionality to achieve what your heart desires. Let's be clear, though. That mental revelation shouldn't be the thing that discourages you. Your actions already validated that thus far. That's not negative self-talk, that's taking ownership for the role you play in your own fate. Accountability is everything if you want to effectively launch your career after graduation. One of my greatest pet peeves is when individuals do not hold themselves accountable for how certain situations in their life pan out. As you read, I would rather you sit in your truth and say, "I'm not ready… YET" than to place blame on everything and everyone else for why you can't take the first step in the right direction. Once the acknowledgment is there, then reading this book can still be of value to you, but begin to ask yourself why you're not ready. What would motivate you to get ready to take on new practices now to further your success post-undergrad? What barriers are you currently up against? Before you simply stop at your long list of obstacles to use as scapegoats for why you can't achieve your goals, begin to immediately couple possible solutions for those concerns. That's problem-solving at its finest. One of the key tenants of this book is to force the deepest self-reflection possible, and by doing so, you can better identify strategies to be successful *figuring shit out* after college.

Despite my rather blunt nature, if you need a pocket of motivation, a snippet of prayer, and a gentle reminder that you were put on Earth to fulfill great things, I'm your girl and this book is for you. I hope my tools will grant you with a greater sense of guidance to pair with an already existing Christ-like discernment, not because you may or may not know specifically which career you are supposed to enter, but because you stand firm in knowing you were called by God to be great. Be excited for what the future holds *if* you do the work.

I wrote this book with the specific intention to keep it plain with you—so let me be clear from the beginning. I can share my tips with how I landed my first job within my field of study fresh out of college, but by no means will I imply that you will fall in love with your position or land your dream job to start. I am not promising that you will love your boss or even land a job that is a good fit for you or the employer. By no stretch of the imagination, do I even want you to think that by possibly changing your major or shifting careers in a field other than what you studied is an indicator that you are failing or not walking in your purpose. All these things you learn when developing your career. Using myself as an example, I didn't need a degree to write this book per se. However, it was my experiences in higher education that were necessary for this book to come to fruition. This book is more than a guide for other scholars, but a task I believe I was called to do based on my experiences collectively. My hope for you is that the time you are investing in school is putting you one step closer to recognizing your calling. You will have to do things you don't like to better understand what you enjoy and can see yourself doing long-term. No one is exempt from paying their dues, especially as a young and eager individual with little to no experience, hoping and praying that a job seeker will even look at your resume. Trust and believe when you get your start in the workforce after undergrad, employers have mastered taking advantage of that drive. Along your journey, you may very well be worked to the bone for laughable pay to start, have to uproot and relocate to an unfamiliar place (as I did), and work for employers who will have you thoroughly convinced that they are the spawn of Satan who operate the organization in the most illogical way possible. Regardless, you must hone in on the fact that this is all a part of your *destined process*.

I pray that God will bless you with an employer who will have the actual skillset and environment to take you under their wings and groom you to be the best associate you can be. I pray that your pay will increase exponentially. I pray your first job opportunity after college affords you top-notch learned skillsets that will be forever transferrable in your next career-based opportunity. I pray that you fall in love with God's obstacles to prepare you for your *destined process*, especially in times of workplace turmoil. I pray that your light shines brightest in the office or the field, so that not only might your hard work consistently be recognized and rewarded, but that consumers begin to ask for you by name!

Now, I can pray this over your life and give my strongest regards, but a prayer is only as good as the time and energy you are willing to invest, both physically and spiritually. As the old saying goes, *prayer doesn't work unless you do*. As God has consistently shown in all of our lives, a prayer is good, but you've got to be properly equipped with the weapons to fight. With that, I encourage you to keep reading to add to your weaponry, as this is not just an educational walk, but a spiritual war.

Introduction

"Oh shit." Two words that haunted me my last year and a half of college. Between working two jobs to put myself through school and gaining internship experience, while also juggling a full-time course load, I had run myself ragged to have a plan, and ensure all ducks were aligned so that my post-undergrad transition was bulletproof. I often let those two words consume the majority of my day and rob me of my sleep, peace, and joy. Now, I know this may not be the most pleasant way to start my book, with the intentions of it being to motivate and encourage, but it is *my* start. This is the reality of my backstage prayers and worries that have unfolded into the onstage blessings that you see today. Life has a way of leaving us confused during certain periods in our lives, and it's only with time that we can look back and reflect on why God put us through what He did. So, as hard as I pushed myself in college— sometimes unnecessarily—it wasn't until I finished school and landed a job within my field that God made it all clear to me. Upon completion of my academic milestone, God spoke to me. He was doesn't with me yet. He said my assignment was not fulfilled. In that moment, I accepted my college journey was not simply for me, but a testimony to be shared to help others. That's when I told my mom about the concept of this book. I had a burning desire to do this, not merely to call myself an author, but because I felt it was a spiritual requirement that God placed on my heart. If anyone knows a thing or two about spiritual requirements, then they know they have a funny way of radiating over your thoughts until you make a move. Another thing that I've learned about spiritual requirements is that when you become aware of what you are called to do, life has a way of showing you tons of signs that reinforce your assignment. For example, I enjoyed watching new movies and shows by random selection. I didn't think it was a coincidence that the lead character was either an established or aspiring author or some renowned book publisher. At one point when writing this book, I gave the show *Jane the Virgin* a chance. When I was struggling to find the time to write, in the television series, Jane too, was also struggling to find time to write her book because of the many directions life was pulling her in. Like Jane, for the most part, whenever I did find the time to write my book, I was Usain Bolt on my keyboard. God has probably done something similar to you while in college—giving you confirmation of your destined path without you even taking heed to it. Pay attention to those signs since they are there to help you *figure shit out*.

The majority of my friends have always been a few years older than me, including those in college. While in undergrad, I would have casual conversations with my older counterparts, inquiring about their plans as they were soon approaching graduation. Needless to say, none of them had it all figured it, which was fine, but many of them also didn't have a sense of direction as to their next move either. This is a trap that many college students fall into. Granted, I can understand those who may say life is about the journey and not the destination, but let's be real; you had four-plus years to have some sense of direction. If not, essentially, college was a royal waste of time. At the minimum, college should have ruled out what you didn't want to do, and also afforded you opportunities to explore your options beyond the scope of the classroom. If you chose not to maximize the opportunities of academic and career exploration, then that's on you (which we will discuss in a later chapter).

When I asked many of my friends and college associates who were a few months shy of graduating had they begun applying for jobs within their field, maybe only two out of the twenty said they had. This baffled me since most of them were complaining about how difficult it was to get a job out of college, let alone a job within their field. Coupling my encounters with college counterparts and my research on job placement statistics, the more stunned I became. According to a 2013 Washington Post article, "27 percent of college grads had a job that was closely related to their major." At first glance,

I interpreted the statistic as being an economic issue and lack of job opportunities. As I continued to dig deeper, even branching out by making inquiries to students from other colleges, a greater, more unspoken truth was that many college students weren't doing what was necessary to prepare themselves for job placement while in college. Often, it boiled down to students not actively applying themselves (beyond tests and term papers), both figuratively and literally!

Let me be clear by acknowledging that many college students have extensive responsibilities such as taking care of children or siblings, traveling long distances to get to class, or in some instances, working grueling hours to support their families. Under these circumstances, it makes complete sense why a few late arrivals and early class departures are necessary. My book is not focused on those more intimate variables that could naturally impact one's ability to attend school. My objective in writing this book was not to come from a damaged center belief system—placing sole blame on the subjects for these conditions. I also want to note that I know firsthand, the negative impacts associated with damage-centered research, being the subject of it myself as a person of color consistently compared to White achievement. I can personally attest to the flaws in this primarily White space we call education. That is a topic for another book. However, living these experiences have also acted as fuel to help me better navigate academia (a system that wasn't designed with my Black ass in mind) and come up with strategies to ensure long-term success. This book addresses the average college student who may not be considering or taking advantage of the opportunities built into the cost of attendance.

I knew at the start of my junior year it was time to make revisions to my standard college routine by actively considering my life after finishing school. I went into overdrive ensuring my grades were solid, applying for internships related to my fields of study, and all other standard college practices. I consistently made strides to seize every opportunity that would make my job search easier. Despite feeling overwhelmed with my studies at times, applying for jobs while still enrolled eliminated the societal pressures that come with starting at ground zero as soon as you graduate. At times I put unhealthy amounts of pressure on myself to make sure I had some kind of game plan after graduating, but that force is also the very thing that lit a fire under my ass to do things differently than the average graduating senior. My academic objective wasn't simply to graduate. I made a vow to myself to explore as many opportunities afforded to me in college because I never wanted to question what I should have done to further my career. And now, I look forward to sharing my life lessons with you, with hopes that with a few changes in your habits and routine, you too, can land that job after school within your field of study.

Chapter 1
Understand Your Drive

Theory for Reflection

> "Self-determination theory (SDT) assumes that inherent in human nature is the propensity to be curious about one's environment and interested in learning and developing one's knowledge."
>
> - (Niemiec and Ryan, 2009)

I knew when God tasked me with the responsibility to write this book, I couldn't give readers the superficial steps of what they should do in their life without evaluating mine. Before I could even define what my steps were in college to land a job within my field, it required that I reflected on my needs. If I was going to come up with a course of action for my life, I needed to understand what I was working toward. What was I doing all of this for? That is the question I constantly asked myself, and also urge you to consider to better grasp the concepts of this book.

What's your drive? That's a common question in academia, especially in guidance courses. While I believe it's a valid question, I also think it's loaded. If you can't come up with some beautifully constructed, politically correct answer to the question, people tend to look at you funny. Trust me, I tried to answer that bullshit ass question time and time again. The harder I tried to best verbalize what drove me, the more tongue-tied I became. I especially felt the pressure since I always made it a point to carry myself with poise and dignity when delivering myself to people when I spoke. By making the constant attempt to "show my best face," outsiders automatically subscribed to the notion that I could effortlessly answer any question; questions, by the way, that many of them can't answer for their damn self. While my immediate flesh wanted to quickly respond to the infamous, "What drives you?" question with, a simple, "I just am," after further considering it, that response isn't accurate.

It was never one specific factor that was the driving force behind my diligence and desire to put in the work to succeed. When I accepted this, I knew I would never be able to answer that question concisely. As I continued to live my life, I came to understand that motivation is fluid for everyone. Whether that be school, work, medical bills, having children to feed, or not having parents to financially depend on, life will present its fair share of never-ending challenges, none of which should be an excuse as to why goals can't be achieved. The sooner you realize it will never be just one thing that's disrupting your flow, the better off you will be. All of life's stressors are the forces behind your drive. When I came to terms with that, I stopped answering that question. I stopped forcing myself to try and come up with some cookie cutter answer to describe my drive, when I was living in the same imperfect world as everyone else. My drive, like yours, boils down to what we are consistently exposed to. As cliché as is sounds, since I wasn't satisfied with every condition I experienced, I took steps to change it.

One of the most influential factors in all our lives is family. It doesn't take being a psychologist to understand how the sociological unit significantly affects the way we go about life. When I think about what I was consistently exposed to growing up, I recall making promises to myself about what I would do differently. Most of what I took issue with revealed itself when I was a kid. The only thing I *could* do as a child was make promises to myself. When I became a young adult, I had the power to actively commit to those promises I made to that little girl all those years ago.

For starters, my parents divorced before I could even remember. I don't divulge that information for sympathy. It's just my starting point. When considering my first pivotal experience in understanding where my drive derived from, it would stem from seeing how hard my mother worked. Like any child emulating their parent's behavior, that same work ethic became prevalent in my adult life. Being raised by a single mother gave me a front-row seat to witness a black woman hustle like no other. I admired my mom so much as a little girl. She had a big, beautiful Colgate smile everyone loved. She was stunning as she dressed up for work with her *Halle Berry* short hairstyle and perfectly manicured nails. She was such a hard worker, effortlessly demonstrating grace every step of the process. She was my *shero*. My mom worked in transportation sales for over twenty years. Anyone who knows a thing or two about the industry will tell you it's not for the weak or for dummies. Her dedication to work radiated even more as she was the only black women at her company and one of the highest-grossing sales associates. Not to mention, she primarily worked in Orange County. If you aren't familiar with the area, it is one of the wealthiest counties in Southern California, meaning it was a competitive market for the very seasoned sales professionals. As a teeny-bopper, it was always evident to me that the harder she worked, the more unmatchable her hustle truly was. My mother managed to achieve a great deal of success, all without a college degree. Before I lose you as a reader, since this book is to encourage you to actively pursue higher education to best land a job after graduating, remember that times are much different now and require far more. It's up to you to keep up with the times. I'll talk more about this in a bit.

Since my mom's work demanded so much of her time, naturally, I saw less of her than the average elementary student. As you can imagine, it wasn't always easy being seven, eight, and nine years old and your mom walking in your room at five in the morning to say, "Bye. Have a good day at school," and not returning home until six or seven in the evening. Even with that, I always remained understanding that she had to work to provide for two kids.

For the most part, I was responsible for setting my alarm clock and getting myself ready and off to school. If I wasn't in the after-school program, I was at home finishing homework, bathing, and making sure the chicken was taken out of the freezer. Although I had my Auntie Chonie throughout this journey as well, it didn't change my young thought process—do what was required of me even if the circumstances weren't ideal for a child. While my mom made a nice living for our family, it required everyone to step up, even this then nine- or ten-year-old girl. My mother was also caring for my then toddler-aged sister as well. She had work in one hand and my sister in the other. This didn't sadden me when I was younger, but as I grew up, I realized that by having to play a part in my own raising, there was a shift in my biological and sociological wiring to figure shit out and get shit done. It wasn't because I wanted to. There simply wasn't another option. Looking back though, I believe with her working as hard as she did, and her mom passing when she was only eleven years old, it left some disconnects in her ability to show gentle and affectionate motherly love. *The grind* was the only language she understood, leaving much of her maternal instincts out of sync. With that, she was extremely hard on me growing up. This was during my formative years of understanding what it means to be a "big girl." This was a time when I had no other choice but to become self-sufficient because caring for myself was a direct correlation in helping my mom.

In 2008, everything changed. Not only did the recession hit, but shit hit the fan. My mom, like millions of others, was laid off. Like all of us, I'm sure my mom had demons she was battling long before the recession, but when thinking long and hard about the dynamic between my mother and me, this time frame was when I realized how important healthy communication was. She is the reason why I value communication so much to this day. During that time, I think my mom was so fixated on proving the point that everything she earned was self-made that when she lost the financial means to support us at the same capacity, it enhanced her frustration and irritability with people, including her children. During this time, jobs were sparing. The constant conversations that my mom had in the corner that she thought I didn't see between her and the mortgage lenders ensued. I admired her efforts though as she tried to make every attempt to downplay how bad her financial state was by telling me not to worry, but I knew. I could feel the tension all throughout the house. If anything, I was probably more susceptible to the nervous energy as a child.

Despite the financially trying years ahead, miraculously, my mom still managed to keep our home. As times slowly started to change and jobs became available, one distinct requirement appeared more consistently on job postings, a bachelor's degree—the piece of paper so many people praise, but the very thing that acted as a thorn in my mom's side. As our current workplace reality marks, while employers want you to have lengthy work experience, many recruiters will bypass your resume if you don't have the degree to back it up. It didn't matter how extensive my mom's experience was. Without the degree, this "new age" workforce left her in for a rude awakening, navigating uncharted territory. I think as the intensity of the job hunt weighed on my mom, it made it that much harder for her to show a softer sider at home. I found that the more stressed she became, the harder she was on me. That firecracker came out. Firecrackers never apologize for the damage and destruction their impact causes. They just expect everyone around them to exercise caution. She was reckless with her words, lacked patience, and didn't seem to care about the hurt she inflicted. As she was going through her battles and I was coming into my own as a teenager, naturally, we started to have even greater issues. Even with our problems, I remained dedicated to my studies, with hopes it would please her and improve her mood. It never seemed like enough, though. If anything, the more I thrived in grade school, the more unimpressed she was. To her, it was an expectation that I performed exceptionally well, so she wasn't one to really give accolades, at least not privately. While everyone else doted over me for my work ethic in school and everything in between, they didn't know I was doing it all to appease the most difficult critic, my momma. She's slowly coming around though, respecting that this isn't the best way to maintain healthy relationships; but like a firecracker, when the pressures of life are felt, no one around her is safe.

I always valued education for myself, but my mother also made it evident that attending college was, "Not a fucking option." In other words, there was an expectation to attend regardless of what her financial state was. Being a first-generation college student, neither my mother nor I knew how to navigate the realm of academia. We didn't know how we were going to afford it. Even with no sense of clarity, our conversations about me attending college never wavered. In fact, during this time, she was *more* adamant about me obtaining my degree because she saw how costly it was not having hers. I saw how emotionally and professionally taxing it was for her to once be at the top of her game and then disqualified, all because she didn't have a bachelor's degree. In seeing her carry that burden, I not only was ready for college, but received a newfound sense of rejuvenation after experiencing some burn out from the K-12 system. I was determined to abide by that old saying when it came to my degree: "I would rather have it and not need it, than need it and not have it."

My relationship with my mother posed new challenges when I started attending college. Being the first in my family to go to school created an extra layer of anxiety and stress for two reasons. One, just pursuing postsecondary education was a new experience. Two, my circle of people who truly understood the mental, physical, and emotional demands associated with attending school reduced significantly, including a disconnect with my mother. While my mom had always been the primary advocate for me to pursue education, as I began to evolve, come into my own woman, and adhere to my own philosophies of life, at times, it created friction between us. I was actively and purposely living out the self-determination theory listed at the beginning of this chapter. Being in college enticed my curiosity about the world and the people around me. I was eager to break away from some of the dispositions learned in the household and make my own assumptions about life. Unfortunately, that came with a major price to pay in the form of extensive ridicule from the same woman who drilled education into my psyche. Why?

To my surprise, the more consistent I became with focusing on my purpose, the harsher my mom's remarks toward me were. There I was, doing everything that my mom ever asked of me, just to be met with comments reeking of negativity like, "Oh, you think you know everything," and, "I've got something on you—life skills—something them books will never be able to teach you." I would turn my wheels trying to figure out why her ability to inflict pain could roll off her tongue so effortlessly as I was doing the very thing she told me I had to do. I was already going to hear that shit from the world, I did not need to hear that from my mom. What aggravated me more than anything was that my awards, medals, certificates, and acknowledgments were all great bragging rights for her to pull out her back pocket to display to the public, yet at times, I was living a private hell of her breaking me down behind closed doors. Digging deeper and getting older, I started to see her without the "mom" label. She was a woman capable of making mistakes. Someone who may not apologize for her poor behavior. A hurt person hurting other people, taking jabs at the most sensitive and accessible target to her—me.

While we were at odds, I had to remind myself that no matter what flew out her mouth, my mom always wanted me to pursue an education. Like other families with similar issues, sometimes parents misunderstand or are unfamiliar with altogether, that earning a degree and getting a job is only the superficial layer of furthering your education. Pursuing an education was a means to push myself to level up in every aspect of my life—in my diction, relationships, and being an all-around life learner. I had to actively commit to the self-determination theory during times of turmoil, because in doing so it allowed me to feed my curiosity and never lose sight of my desire to gain new knowledge, even if it threatened my mother and others around me. I had to create the space to unapologetically prioritize myself even if the people around selfishly wrote me off as selfish because I was not at their disposable. I couldn't afford to succumb to anyone else's negativity, even if it was my mother. By doing so, it would interfere in figuring out what my purpose was.

As time passed, my mother admitted to her shortcomings, acknowledging she was somewhat jealous of what I was able to achieve. Although she only mentioned this once and very briefly in my life, it helped put some things in perspective. I learned that sometimes people aren't truly ready for what they ask for. I was focused on school and doing all the things that she outlined to ensure I became *better* than her, but when doing so, she didn't know how to uplift me without being intimidated that I surpassed her. I felt she would take jabs as a way to "humble me" if she felt I was one-upping her, when I was merely trying to level up for myself. Although this made for some unfortunate events in our relationship over the years, that friction was a blessing, a life lesson, a survival test. It acted as the very indicator that I was on track with the plans God set forth for me.

Often, we are taught that only poor behavior warrants unpleasant consequences. However, in my spiritual walk, I've learned that it's the exact opposite. When you are doing what you're supposed to do, that's when massive breakdowns occur in your closest relationships. This was a bittersweet lesson to learn from my mom, but I'm thankful, nonetheless. Momma did say life skills were important, and if it wasn't for her, I would never really know how to be effective at blocking out unnecessary noise while faced with obstacles to keep going toward my destiny.

Next up, Pops. Charming man. He's super outgoing with an infectious energy that keeps people coming back for more. Always the life of the party. He knows everyone, and everyone seems to know him. If you're looking for a carefree, good time, then he's your guy. His remarkable ability to worry less stems from his loving vibrancy that leaves people wanting to swoop in and lend him a helping hand. What can possibly be wrong with that? Anything I say after this will probably sound like complaining, right? I beg to differ, as

I'm merely making observations and reflecting on the aspects of my life that make me unique and drive me to maximize my opportunities. Just like my mother, my relationship with my father is a major determining factor to understand why I feel the need to grind so hard in every aspect of my life. As wonderful as his traits are for everyone else, as his child, this often left me feeling like the adult in our relationship, having to always problem-solve—doubling that sense of urgency to mature faster on top what I was already experiencing from my mom. My dad couldn't grasp that, leaving us with major emotional disconnects and communication gaps over the years.

While most days I admire my dad's ability to stop worries right in their tracks and be a free spirit without any consideration of his future, these aren't ideal traits for a parent who's truly adhering to their responsibilities. My dad always found a way to just be content at whatever stage of life he was in. When I think of a true go-getter, Pops isn't at the top of my list, but he has other talents that carry him. While it would be unreasonable to expect everyone to have an entrepreneurial spirit, as I was growing up, I often felt that my dad missed the mark in having the grit to go out and provide for his kid by any means necessary. Naturally, I felt a greater sense of expectation from him, not because my mother said anything that would sway my views of him, but just by way of seeing her carry the financial load alone.

I knew that asking my dad for anything growing up was a royal waste of time. He would always find some reason why he couldn't match the level of contribution from my mom. First, he would say, he would come through, just to pull the rug from underneath my little feet. Then he blamed me because I didn't give him enough "notice," followed by me needing to "let him know in advance," which to no surprise was never enough notice for him. When I was about twelve or thirteen years old, I stopped asking for his help. This is the primary reason why I felt the need to start working at a very young age. When I got a bit older, I got a job, accepting his inability to come through, while alleviating some financial strain from my mom as she was going through her financial woes. I stopped walking toward what I knew would be a disappointment on the other side by going to him, just to enter adulthood and be criticized by the same man because I actively chose not to believe in him due to his track record. This isn't to say there was no contribution at all from him along the way, but it was never enough to make me feel like I could stop worrying about finances as a child when I saw my mom constantly making a way out of no way. This is when I started to painfully witness and learn that women, especially Black women, often must do the heavy lifting and adjust to life's unfortunate odds. My dynamic with my parents unfortunately, perpetuated a common stigma within the Black community—I couldn't trust a man to do the heavy lifting and it was on me to get things done no matter what. Obviously, I'd be lying if I said this didn't negatively impact many of my relationships and not just romantic ones. However, these experiences still planted valuable seeds that I carried into undergrad. I was going to make this degree work for me by any means necessary because I couldn't bank on anyone else to ensure the college route would play in my favor.

Despite being an adult, not seeking support from anyone, this is still a sore spot that my father and I constantly butt heads about. To this day, sometimes I feel that my dad faults me for not believing in him, even though we both know he can't contribute. Although I'm far beyond looking for anyone to take care of me, I think it pains him that I have made peace with not relying on him. His actions taught me that no matter how incapable you know that man to be, every man must feel needed. That's extremely difficult for independent women, not just because of our ability to self-serve, but because we are often *forced* to be independent. So, to a degree, I can understand why he gets upset when I ignore his *promises*. My dad still yearns for that little girl with big brown eyes to look up and entrust him to sweep me off my feet when I can't bear the weight of the world, all while simultaneously demonstrating that he's the one that needs most of the carrying. He taught me at a very young age that dependability, not just from a man, but from anyone, was a privilege, not a right. The only guarantee I could bank on was myself. While I got really good at casually dismissing his façade of support, we both knew the reality, and we both knew how frustrated I got behind it. To be clear, it stopped bothering me years ago that he couldn't really support. It irked me that he invested half of his energy saying he would help me and expelled the other half of his energy attempting to save face with family, at times, falsely shouting that he was supporting when most people knew he wasn't. He just missed the mark.

It sucks ass that most of what I learned from my father never came easy. Fed up, trying to express my disappointment of how he made me feel, I was met with a condescending cop out talking about, "At least you learned something, Alexis." I hate that it always had to be a damn struggle. He didn't teach me to let a man open my door. He didn't teach me to allow someone to do something nice for me, like take me out to dinner. He didn't teach me to let a man pick up the check or pull my chair out for me. He didn't teach me the value of a man being a financial provider. Sometimes I felt he would deliberately go out his way to not support me, yet always mustered up enough boldness to inquire about my finances when it was rarely to add to my pocket. This man could fix his lips to "jokingly" ask me for money along my broke college student journey, without any intention to contribute to my well-being despite being made fully aware of how financially strapped I was. Between working two jobs and attending school full-time, in addition to having to be the adult in the daddy-daughter relationship, my patience was waning, and my exhaustion was setting.

I remember expressing the feelings of hurt to my Uncle Curtis, my dad's best friend, and a church deacon. While he profusely reiterated his love for my dad, he shared something that will forever stick with me. He said, "Baby, sometimes men get comfortable. We want to plant our seeds in this world, but don't necessarily do everything to tend to them. As men, we get spoiled because we know our *baby mamas* are just going to come through and take care of it. It doesn't make it right… but that's why you have to be careful with who you have kids with." After leaving me with pearls of wisdom, as he always does, he breaks the seriousness of our conversation and yells, "You know your dad is crazy," and burst out laughing with his deep Black Santa voice.

Shortly after my grandfather passed away, my dad and I were fighting, most likely over the same behavior of all of our father-daughter dismay. I was driving in my car infuriated, agitated by his eagerness to constantly clock my pockets to only be nosey without any intent to help. In the midst of my anger, I heard my grandfather speak to me. He said ever so clearly, "Baby, I didn't understand what I should have known then until after I passed on." At that moment, the tension in my shoulders melted away and acceptance kicked in. My family always said my granddad and Pops are just alike, especially in their mannerisms. My granddad knew I needed to hear and feel him at that moment. When he was alive, I could always count on him to make me laugh no matter how upset I was. Unfortunately, I couldn't laugh at that moment. I was angry with his son. My granddad's words were his way of saying he was just like my dad. Whether

I saw it or not, it didn't change the fact that they were birds of the same feather. While I don't wish any harm upon my dad, those precious words from the other side were telling me that even if my dad tried, he would never be able to truly understand the hurt he inflicted on me until after he crossed over.

Granddad's words reminded me that I had a choice. I could continue to view my dad with disappointment or accept that in this life, this was as good as it will ever get with him. The kicker is, granddad never said I had to condone my dad's behavior. Knowing how much my granddad loved me and admired my strength and unwavering ability to stand my ground, he wouldn't want me to. He did, however, allow me to accept that as people, we may never change in this lifetime, but will only have the capacity to truly understand our flaws once when we stand before Christ. In the meantime, I will love my parents for who they are while continuing to be unapologetic in setting boundaries, as I am certain they would want me to practice in all my relationships.

Speaking of boundaries, they are a necessity for all healthy relationships. Boundaries help define and redefine your self-worth, especially in your closest relationships. While this may come as a shocker to some, your father and mother are not exempt from moral expectations because they brought you in this world. These are the first people who teach us how we are to be treated. Establishing boundaries showed me that the people who are accustomed to violating them tend to guilt trip you when you set them. The audacity of me! Such blasphemy that I could protect my peace of mind and prioritize my mental health. The nerve of me to choose my wellness. The dishonor I bring to practice self-care that boundary crossers said I needed so much, yet never minded when I sacrificed my mental and physical health if it meant dropping everything to help them. But I digress. All of this connects to my achievements post-undergrad because in setting boundaries with those close to me, not just my parents, it required that I loved myself enough to create a space where I could best thrive.

For the longest time, anger drove me. Disappointment drove me. The promise I made to little Alexis all those years ago to never rely on a man for shit is what drove me! Money drove me. Stability drove me. Then, after I had all these come-to-Jesus moments, I had an epiphany. While I found myself confused time and time again over my dad's "fatherly" methods, the greatest lesson he taught me turned out to be synonymous with the motions I witnessed my mom go through all those years. The lesson? Other than God, I had no one to take care of me or nothing to fall back on. That was enough to push me to thrive by any means necessary. Looking back, I guess that would also qualify as the best answer to that infamous question of what drives me. I saw a post on social media that said, "Nobody works harder than a MF who hates asking people for shit." That's me. I'm that MF.

It took years of reflection on my end to come to understand that my parents are only human. It doesn't mean I have zero expectations of them, because I most certainly do, just as they hold for me as their daughter. What changes is the expectations that I place on myself to consistently strive for something more because there wasn't a safety net to cradle my fall. I don't share this part of my life to throw my parents' history in their face or to deliberately publicize it, but when considering the various factors that make me uniquely Alexis Thrower, it came with accepting that my truest motivation to succeed all stemmed from life's ugliest realities, even if some of them came from my loved ones. Maybe that was the blessing in it all. The thicker my skin became from my family, the easier it was to cope with outsiders, those I cared nothing about. It was up to me to take these dark moments and never use them as a crutch or excuse. I have to always hold myself accountable for my actions and create something beautiful from it. I must do this all while unapologetically letting my light shine as I'm figuring it all out in the process.

For your next reflection, I want you to think about your life. Consider all the current factors that put a sense of pressure on you to succeed. Give it some thought. There's no wrong answer.

_____
_____
_____
_____
_____

Chapter 2
Know Your Purpose and Stay Focused

There's no real theory to help determine what your purpose is in life. Everyone comes to that revelation through an assortment of ways. Some people just know their purpose and confidently walk in it from birth. Others have no clue. To understand what your purpose is requires consistently exposing yourself to different experiences, especially those afforded to you while in college. This is an opportunity to hone in on your strengths and weaknesses, as those are telltale signs of what you should focus on and steer clear of.

From the tender age of six, I swore I wanted to be a pediatrician. It wasn't until I was in high school and realized I didn't like science, and science didn't like me. It simply didn't click. Discouraged, I gave up that "dream." Fighting an internal battle, I had to relinquish this vision I had for my life and accept the fact that I didn't need to have it all figured out in the tenth grade.

I was always a worrier growing up. I'm still guilty of it at times. And yes, as a Christian girl, I know that goes against everything they taught me in church when it comes to giving my problems to God. Newsflash though, I'm human as well and I'm sure when God created me, he knew I would be a natural stressor. I believe much of my stress stemmed from wanting to have a plan established and sticking to it— very much a type A personality. Even to this day I've never made it a habit to follow a plan B because I am used to being methodical in my thinking for plan A to pan out accordingly. My first plan always had to work. That's how I approached the medical field and pediatrics. It was something that I was going to force fit in my life because I wasn't open-minded to anything else. I had great doctors as a kid, I loved playing with the equipment while I waited for the medical professionals to come in the exam room—even if my mom withheld the fact that I was getting a shot that visit. Even as a budding child myself, I remember having an immense love for kids. Perfect profession, right? Think again. I started taking high school biology, chemistry, and physics and was miserable. I got massive stress-related headaches fighting to retain the material. I would get frustrated at the thought of having to tackle science classes well before they even started. I felt defeated. This was not the field for me, which was scary to face because students in this day and age are under far greater pressure than what it used to be. We are no longer groomed to work one job at one company for the rest of our lives. We are expected to be the best, demonstrate the best, and have a greater sense of direction of where we are going, because if not, the older generations will jump down our throats for not taking advantage of all the opportunities they didn't have back in their day. I would even argue that the pressure is felt more for students of color, succumbing to the double standards of what it means to be exceptional in every aspect of your life to prove you don't fit stereotypical molds in the classroom, the corporate world and in the family unit. What the hell was next for me with what felt like the weight of the world on my back?

Like most students working their way through the ranks, trying to figure out what direction they were going to take after high school, I was often met with remarks along the lines of, "Oh, don't worry about it, you have two years to complete your college prerequisites to figure it out." In my case, this wasn't the least bit reassuring, as many of them didn't know, let alone did I have the energy to repeat, that I was enrolled in a program that allowed me to take college courses starting my junior year of high school. When I walked across the stage to gather my high school diploma, I already had a year's worth of prerequisites completed. So those funky ass two years people harped on, was not the case for me. I only had one year to have some kind of plan so I did not waste my time. I only had one year to ensure that wonderful financial aid money didn't go to waste for a degree I wasn't going to use. This was exhausting and too much for one person to keep up with.

I can recall these feelings and anxious emotions like it was yesterday. I remember being a bundle of nerves approaching the eleventh grade, living in constant doubt, trying to make sense of what my calling was, because I thought

I knew all along. The insecurity associated with not knowing what was next for my life rattled me. It's one thing to have no sense of direction of where you want to go in life, but it's an even worse feeling when life slaps you in the face and tells you everything you *thought* was your purpose turned out to be a pipe dream. To this day I think I would have loved being a pediatrician, but I don't believe I would have *made it* to see it come to fruition. Whatever the specifics of that may mean, I'm not too sure and I haven't given it further thought, but I do know that I would have lost my upbeat nature that attracts people to me in the first place. Throughout this moment of discovery, I had to make peace that there was something else destined for me. However, to find out what that was I had to let go of a childhood dream that I never wavered from. It was time for me to allow life to reveal what I was truly supposed to do.

After dissecting my high school experiences with other professionals and going back into the community and speaking with other high school students, I've pinpointed one of the greatest flaws of our kindergarten through twelfth-grade system. Many students select professions in close proximity to what they see on a daily basis or on television. They opt for careers such as doctor, police officer, teacher, dentist. Many schools don't even budget for field trips anymore. This is a major equity issue which in turn, spills over into college life, making it more difficult for young adults to have the foundation to figure shit out.

At six years old, I selected pediatrics as my profession because I had a great pediatrician who I saw consistently. If kids are only exposed to their general scope of understanding, this cripples young minds long-term who have no clue about the hundreds of thousands of professions they have to choose from, or better yet, the ones they can create. Even though I became a journalist, while in high school I didn't know what the definition of a "journalist" was or that I could become one, despite doing extracurricular activities synonymous with the job role. I honestly didn't even explore the depth of the profession until my freshman year of college. I remember seeing those people on television talking about sad stuff. I recall my grandfather telling me how important it was to always know what was going on in the world as he sat on the couch or in bed flicking through all the local news stations. Yet, I didn't see the *sad news people's* value, and I certainty wasn't watching them given that Disney Channel was more appropriate for my attention span at the time. Although I was exposed to seeing the people on television deliver news material, no one explained this as a possible profession. To me, newscasters were just people on another program to flick through while channel surfing. The is another issue with our K-12 system. If students happen to entertain a profession outside of their everyday purview, they often pick something that sounds good without any additional research about what the job truly entails. For example, I spoke with some high school students who said they wanted to major in engineering. I'd further ask them what type of engineer they wanted to be. They could hardly provide me with any details. They didn't know the difference between mechanical, electrical, industrial, chemical, and civil engineers. They picked what *sounded* good. They're not to blame, though. As a society, we expect late teenagers and early 20-year-olds to have some sense of direction by the time they make it to a university, but don't equip them with a wider knowledge base to explore opportunities they never knew existed. This is exactly why I was insecure to apply for college with an "undeclared" major.

I originally got accepted at California State University, Los Angeles, as a psychology major, not because I was interested in psychology, even though I did take a psych class and enjoyed it, but because I did not want to chance applying to colleges as undeclared and being viewed as not knowing how to tackle college, despite every education professional telling me that it was okay to do so. I knew all along that I was a much stronger extrovert communicator than interpersonal listener to someone else's problems in a quiet office, yet no one was having the conversation with me about how to translate this knowledge into a career that best suited my strengths to gain steady income.

We continue to preach that children are our future, yet only a small fraction of us go back and volunteer, mentor, teach, and speak to our youth. From there, kids go on to college rightfully declared as "undecided" for their major with no real basis of what they want to do, and without any exposure to careers that they *think* they want to do. Then students must learn a completely new academic routine, from enrolling in their own classes, taking different courses every few months, and handle lingering student account balances because if they don't, they run the risk of being dropped from their classes! God forbid they're still trying to learn the ropes of this new environment and fall in love with Ms. Jada's son who turns out to be a hot ass mess of a distraction along the way! I know from experience. Shit happens! Nonetheless, that's a lot to handle, and as a community, we must better expose our children to as many opportunities as we can while they're young, so they have a greater sense of direction and confidence when they approach college. By investing in them early, we better encourage young scholars to pursue higher education purposefully because they have a clear vision of where they are going, or at the minimum, know how to best navigate through trial and error.

Parents, listen to what your kids are saying when they express their interests, even if it consistently changes, and start seeking out opportunities to expose them to that profession. You would be surprised what a few phone calls could get you. If you are a business owner, for example, open your establishment to kids considering entrepreneurship. Whether they are volunteering or getting community service credit, this is the remedy to helping our youth find their purpose. For any high school students reading this, one, it's not too early to apply the concepts in this book for your life, and two, take advantage of the head start you have now by calling local organizations to see if you could observe for a week or ask questions to one of the professionals. Use LinkedIn to connect with people in your dream profession, or at least the profession you *think* is your dream job. Maybe you have some general understanding about what you like doing but have no idea which major will be beneficial to your career. These are conversations that should be happening well before you ever step foot on anybody's college campus. You may be in a situation like myself and come to the realization you've been walking in your purpose all along. What good is that though if you don't have the necessary exposure to various experiences to be sure?

Before I share more about stepping into my purpose, let's take a second to decompress. I know you have personally felt some of the pressures of society fall on your shoulders when it comes to your life. Sometimes, those thoughts are so heavy, it clouds our judgment by creating doubt and fear. I know because those were the two feelings I battled with for the longest time. Right now, give yourself permission to let it go! I want you to jot down some of the comments people have said to you about what you should do with your life. Write down your doubts and fears. What have you been naturally good at all these years? What's the thing you try over and over again and still can't get right? Think about what the younger you could have used to find their path knowing what you know now. While doing this exercise, I hope you stop letting these mental manifestations affect your present and give yourself a blank canvas so that clarity in your calling finds you.

Although I had permitted myself to let go of a childhood dream, I still wanted to have a productive plan for my life. Even though I received financial aid, whether it was my money or someone else's, I respected that time is of the essence. By *responsibly* relinquishing my vision for what I *thought* I was supposed to do with my life, I had unlocked the door that God had been waiting for me to enter—to move over and let Him step in to reveal the plan He has for me.

When I've shared the concept to others about responsibly relinquishing my vision, I was often met with a deaf ear or frown from my college counterparts, so allow me to elaborate.

I get it! You're in college just taking one step in front of the other. Maybe you're burnt out with the educational process. I mean you have been in school since kindergarten, and that's not including Pre-K education. This is twelve plus years of pure and rightful exhaustion. Your freshman year of college passes. Then your sophomore year. You're just… there… going through the motions. This in itself, was one of the number one observations I made from my college colleagues. Many of them were simply fixed on "getting the hell out of there" that they didn't plant the necessary seeds to give themselves a crop to pick from post-college to help land the job within their field. Responsibly relinquishing the plans for yourself means, in plainest terms, not becoming a leach, couch potato, a bum… whichever word you need to strike that chord on the inside of you. It's about exercising responsibility while remaining productive as you're figuring things out. Responsibly relinquishing your plans means you're being open to what life has in store for you, but not growing complacent with where you are—setting micro goals, major goals, and connecting with the right people to help you figure out what's next.

While college affords many opportunities, it can also be a dangerous trap that breeds complacency, because of the routine that post-secondary education presents us. Most college students have a set schedule, work part-time around classes, and participate in extracurricular activities such as sports, that also fill in gaps for designated amounts of time. Our lives are essentially planned out for the next four years or so. Although I personally swear by a schedule to give my life some structure, if not careful, we begin to merely go through the motions of college. It gets easier to let go of being intentional with your time. You are less likely to be proactive in laying the foundation for what your life can and will look like after college. It's during this window of time that some college students start to drop out or take a year off to travel with the honest intention to reset and return to school but fail to re-enroll. Along the journey, they misplaced intentionality—the reason they were there in the first place. Once that's gone, what genuine motivation do students have to complete the degree?

For the sake of balancing the scales, taking time off may very well work for some people. I had an instructor advise me to take a year off after completing undergrad to gain work experience before pursuing my master's. This was the route he took, but I chose a different path. I finished undergrad December 2017 and started my graduate program a month later, while gaining work experience simultaneously. Whether you love school or not, it is very easy to fall *out* of the routine of school. Knowing that and myself well enough to understand that I could thug it out going the educational route, I didn't want to take a long break between finishing undergrad and starting my master's program. Different strokes for different folks, though. Either way, exposing yourself to opportunities that are best for you is ultimately *your* responsibility. Even if you wind up hating some of the experiences along your path, this is how you come to understand what your calling is. Do constant check-ins with yourself and remember the basis of your decision-making, which was to solely *figure out* and *live out* what you were called to do. Through all of this, pay attention to your level of discipline in the midst of all of life's temptations. Some people need a year off to best recuperate. I didn't feel much need to. I enjoyed the learning process that an educational institution provided me, and I didn't need a free year or semester to *find myself*, especially when I knew that obtaining my master's degree was always my *minimum* educational goal and that school was the route for me to find out more about who Alexis was.

Still oblivious about what I wanted to do with my life in undergrad, I continued to responsibly relinquish the expectations I placed on myself by finishing my last set of general education courses. One of the last classes I needed was an oral communication course. Every college student must take this course. The class was comprised of preparing and delivering three different speeches. Toward the end of my public speaking course, students considered the work of all of their classmates since the start of the class and selected the best presenter to go on and compete at the speech showcase against presenters of the other oral communication classes. A bit of incentive was that whoever was nominated to deliver their speech on behalf of the class would be exempt from the final presentation. If that student actually won the showcase, their class would get bonus points on their final speech. Needless to say, I was selected to compete and ended up winning the showcase with my speech about academic requirements for student-athletes in comparison to students who didn't play sports.

When the showcase was over, I was interviewed by a student reporter for the university paper. They asked me the standard question. How do you feel about winning the showcase? I told them something along the lines, that this showcase allowed me to understand my greatest fulfillment, which is to use a public platform to express myself and the voices of others. It was at this showcase where my epiphany occurred. God had already been preparing me for this moment and this line of work all my life and I didn't pay attention to any of the signs leading up to it. This was my "ah-ha" moment. This was the purpose defining landmark that not only validated what I loved doing but assured me that I was fulfilling God's plan for my life. It was at that moment I realized that through communication-based concepts, I was meant to change lives.

When I was four years old my mom put me in dance class. I started off taking tap and ballet. As I got older, I continued to develop my artistic craft of dance through an array of styles. Despite not pursuing dance as a career, it has always remained a dear part of my life. Looking back, I can see that God was also using dance as a means to develop my stage presence and find my confidence. As a kid, I was even doing speeches at my church during the Christmas and Easter programs, which kick started experience to a valuable skill that much of the United States population dreads—public speaking. When I was in high school, I performed and hosted the talent show. I even participated in the video production club, which I anchored the weekly campus news—not even knowing that I could make a career out of public speaking. That speech showcase was a means for God to help me recognize my calling and reevaluate my unnecessary stubbornness when holding on to the notion that pediatrics was the only career path for me.

The day following the showcase, I printed out the entire list of my university's majors and minors. While some students are confident in circling their declared major, I took a pen and crossed out every major *I wasn't interested in*. At the end of it, the only two majors that remained were communication and television, film and media studies (TVF) with an option in journalism. In my *naïve* perfect world at the time, I wanted to major in communication and minor in TVF. I later found out that minoring in TVF was not an option at Cal State LA. However, I could do the opposite, and minor in communication and major in TVF. After consulting with my academic advisor, I then inquired about double majoring, which was an even sweeter deal than my intended plan. Given that I was already a year ahead in coursework since I had taken college classes in high school, and many of my college classes were petitioned to double count for both majors, it was a no-brainer. I figured I could graduate in three years with one degree or stay the average four to five years like everyone else and come out with two areas of focus to best market myself. So there I was, in my first year on the university campus, going from not having a clue as to what I was going to major in to double majoring! This came by responsibly relinquishing those strong expectations of working in the medical field, while paying attention to the life lessons along the way. Yes, I had a great deal of uncertainty, but I knew I had to keep taking one step in front of the other until I put the pieces together.

Now for those who don't enjoy school whatsoever, you may be asking yourself, "How do I responsibly relinquish my plans and still find my purpose?" You may be compelled to take an expensive trip somewhere or just work for some time to take a break from the school routine. *Nothing is wrong with that... I repeat... Nothing is wrong with that!* The issue comes into play when you don't establish and stick to the specific intention of why you took that time off in the first place. To avoid complacency in your journey of exploration, I advise you to write down *why* you need the break. Once you've written out your justifications for taking time off, put the document in a place where there is plenty of opportunity for you to come across it. This helps you gently remind yourself that this is a *temporary time of discovery*. Life is all about forever discovery, but in this specific period of rest, you have to set standards to ensure you don't lose sight of your intentions. If not careful, this is how you can get stuck where you are. This time is designed for you to know yourself better in order to accomplish more long-term.

When writing down your needs for a break, assign the amount of time to take off. You must hold yourself accountable for thinking of your next move. If your rest break isn't intentional then neither is the work or lack thereof that will follow. During this time, have some conversations with yourself and God, and when you're halfway through your rest period, reflect on your progress. Have you progressed or have you taken a few steps backward during this time? Putting a timestamp on your break period is just one example of how you responsibly establish what your next step will be or determine if you need to change gears altogether. Without a goal to work toward, momentum is quick to dwindle and hard to get back.

As mentioned earlier, I didn't even realize I was walking in my purpose the entire time, which is the point I want to emphasize to you most. Life will reveal your purpose if you are taking the necessary steps to expose yourself to experiences consistent with learning who you are. When I knew communications and journalism was the route I was supposed to take, I started testing it out for size in conversation. "Hey, Alexis. What's your major and what do you want to do?" I would say, "I'm double-majoring in communication and TVF with an option in journalism. I would love to work in television news as an anchor, reporter, and communication practitioner and instructor." After mingling with hundreds of people throughout my college journey, strangers, acquaintances, and family members alike, quickly interrupted with responses reaffirming my purpose. "Oh yeah! I can see that!" or "I didn't want to say it, but with your look and your delivery even in our conversation now, I know you'll be great at that!" I even heard these same validating remarks from people I met for the very first time. This let me know that others could tell I was walking in my purpose even before I saw it, which was one of the most powerful indicators that I was on the right track.

To get to that place of understanding your calling, you may very well need that breather from school, or plan a getaway trip, or maybe you just keep going through the motions of finishing your prerequisites until you figure it out, but trust that when you have found what you are supposed to do, you will know, and the world will continue to remind you of it!

Chapter 3
Don't Half-Ass Shit

Half-assed: *Defined by Merriam-Webster Dictionary as slang, often vulgar: lacking significance, adequacy, or completeness*

Information foraging theory: *People, when possible, will modify their strategies or the structure of the environment to maximize their rate of gaining valuable information.*

- Peter Pirolli and Stuart K. Card (1999)

Before we go into the specifics of this theory, take a second and think about something. If you had $50,000 right now, what would you do with it? It could be anything. No judgment. Take a moment to jot down a few ideas.

_____
_____
_____
_____
_____

While writing, you may have said buy a car or home, pay off student debt, invest, etc. No matter what you selected, chances are you wanted to maximize the money and the information associated with such goods. Not only did you know what you wanted to do with your cash, but you probably also didn't hesitate. You spent that money without any care of how others would perceive your spending habits. Your actions are in sync with the information foraging theory. While the theory specifically focuses on strategies and technologies for information seeking, gathering, and consumption, it still demonstrates some overlap when it comes to making the necessary modifications in our life to maximize our gain.

While taking the public speaking class during my freshman year of college, at the end of one lecture in particular, my instructor, Mr. Jerrold (pseudonym), somehow ended on the topic of investment. He said, "College is one of the few major sectors where people want and pay more but do so much in their power to receive less." When writing this book, I couldn't help but make a mental association with the information foraging theory. Instead of generally considering the term "people" as the theory suggests, I replaced the phrase with "students." That way it would read, "Students, when possible, will modify their strategies or their structure of the environment to maximize their rate of gaining valuable information." When I rephrased the theory and considered my informal research with my academic colleagues, it became very apparent that many of them would disprove this theory. I started to recognize a commonality within my peers' responses. My college counterparts, I'm sure like many of yours, wanted the job that required the degree within their field, but when asked what their game plan was to make that a reality, many of them had *minimal* basis to validate the chances of that happening.

I valued my initial question at the start of this chapter at $50,000 because a four-year college degree can range anywhere between $30,000 and $50,000, generally speaking. That's not including the extra tuition costs for private, big-named universities or for out-of-state tuition costs. Whether you have financial aid, student loans, or family support, as you already know, education is a major information sector. When considering the information foraging theory, many college students aren't taking advantage of their opportunities beyond the classroom to maximize their gain. We see the memes all the time that make fun of the girl who walks into class late with a Brisk drink and Hot Cheetos, or the classmate who packs their bag and dashes for the door before a formal dismissal. Even with giving those examples, I'm sure your mind started to create a vivid picture of your classmates doing just that, and if not, you're probably the one doing it. These are the people who in some cases (with the exception of students who prearranged their late arrivals and early departures with their professors for private matters), have actively disregarded the academic structure and directly minimized their potential to gain valuable information. If that's the case, it's no wonder why so many graduates are *stuck* after graduating.

When I landed my news producer job, I called my old friend from college to tell him that I got hired. We'll call him Fred. Fred replied, "I'm happy for you, Alexis. To be honest, seeing how hard you worked in college, it doesn't surprise me that you got hired so quickly. Everyone knew you would." Although flattered by these words, it was something else he said later that not only validated I was taking steps in the right direction for my future but was actively building on my knowledge and skillset to help others, even if they weren't ready to receive what I was sharing at the time. Fred graduated about two years before I did, and he was one who I consistently had thought-provoking conversations with. The most powerful thing he said in one of our conversations after I graduated was, "Alexis, looking back, I used to always think that in college you wanted to control my life. I took offense thinking that there was no way this freshman [me] in college knew more about how to handle my life better than I did. Everything you ever said, though, was right. I was just too stubborn to listen." Fred realized that it was not a matter of control that I wanted or needed, as it was me being his accountability buddy. I listened to all the aspirations he had for himself and framed our conversations in a way that forced him to examine what he could do in his present life to get there. Going back to one of the initially introduced concepts of this book, we can pull from anyone's life circumstances independent of gender, age, or any other differentiating characteristic. I was learning what *not* to do from Fred just as much as he was half-listening to me. I wouldn't say Fred did everything wrong because he certainly didn't. However, Fred was one to easily get distracted, having a way of letting his vision of how to utilize his degree take a back seat. I was merely an observer in Fred's life. By watching him and others like him, I was curious. I started to ask a lot of questions. It wasn't for me to judge others, even if that was the perception at times, but to have a greater understanding of their situation, so I could better navigate my own. This aided in my efforts to tailor the college approach I intended on taking by seeing what did and didn't work for other people.

Fred gave me hell for asking him tons of questions, assuming I simply did so to rule his life, unbeknownst to him that I was creating a playbook of my own to ensure my success after college. Because of that, we got into a lot of pointless arguments. He was confident that I was a sparring partner instead of his accountability person. If you are in undergrad, I advise you to find that person who can talk you through your thoughts and dreams and hold you accountable to achieve them. These people can be hard to find so be on the lookout early.

Years later, I realized that Fred taught me a valuable lesson through our tension-filled exchanges. I learned that even as a communication major, despite my ability to find fifty different ways to say the same damn thing, some people aren't ready to receive *what* and *why* you divulge certain information to them. As Fred later admitted, he was in a stage of deflection, assuming that some of the reflective questions I asked could be pushed off until after he graduated, a common belief of many college students. Fred, along with many of my college counterparts deflected about what they knew they needed to do while in college to ensure success post undergrad, lacking consideration about their current surroundings and how some of their present behaviors or the people they may be associating with could be hindering their ability to focus on their goals long-term. That's half-assed behavior, when you don't place enough significance on your long-term priorities. Your short-term priorities and actions reflect that.

Yes, college is meant to me fun and an exciting time of exploration, but like all other spaces, it can be a hub to enable you not to do your best. No need to cut everyone off all together but reevaluate your relationships and reconsider how much time you are dedicating to the ones that aren't helping you live up to your best self. You will have to redefine what your relationships will look like in the future. The wild friend you hold dear to your heart may only get to spend time with you every other weekend. The family members who give you slighted compliments because they can't see your vision may only get your energy once a month. That guy you fell head over hills for and distracts you from your studies may have to take a back seat. If any of these scenarios are applicable to you, then you're not alone. In the interim though, you must find at least one person who will hold you accountable to achieve everything *you said* was a dream of yours. No topic about your life should be off limits to them. This person should be able to speak freely, making you aware of the pitfalls and successes of your personal and professional endeavors.

While you are finding the right partner for you, do not let anyone force themselves to be your accountability partner. Although there is an expectation for people to hold you accountable to some degree, that does not qualify them as your accountability buddy. These are the people who hide behind "saying it like it is" *for them* and not what the experience is like for *you*. Those people also force a connection with extreme differences between your circumstances and theirs as an attempt to validate their credibility to speak freely about your life. Chances are, that self-righteous bullshit is the very reason they are not where they want to be in their own life. Do not waste time faulting them for this, though. When you begin to redefine what your relationships will look like, you will be spending less time with people who do that to you. However, when you find your accountability partner, give them explicit permission to speak on every aspect of your life.

Your accountability partner leads with love—someone who is in a similar situation as you and can speak from true experience to help problem solve and strategize. You must be equally yoked with your accountability partner. It doesn't matter what level you are at in life. Their life goals and intentions align with yours. This is not to be confused with a mentor who is higher in status in your respective field (which we will discuss in a later chapter). Your accountability partner is fighting similar battles as you every day. If anyone can relate to your unique struggle, it's them. They are your supports to help you stay the course of achieving all your heart's desires. Most importantly, your partner reframes your thinking in a manner that uplifts you and always circles back to what needs to be done so you can achieve your goals and vision.

Consider this. If you come across a person who is willing to hold you accountable to achieve your goals but you're defensive, did you give them permission to enter that space? This is a very important question to ask yourself. Even if their line of questioning is on par with aspects of your life that should have been independently considered anyway, were you ready to hear what that person had to say? That's exactly why Fred and I fought. Although Fred harmlessly pushed himself to be a consistent part of my college life, I wrongfully pushed myself onto him as his accountability partner. Fred and I did not explicitly define what that partnership and friendship would look like. I figured if I was working my ass off and someone wanted to share in my space, they too, had to be on their A game. Now, I'll be the first to say that I don't think I'm better than Fred or anyone else for that matter, however, I had a greater hunger to do whatever was necessary to make my degree work for me, even if that meant losing some friends in the process. Many of the people I attended college with were content with superficial relationships—ones that didn't have much substance for long-term professional gain. Fred taught me that everyone isn't looking to keep friends close who push them to be better. That wasn't a bad thing, but if I wasn't careful of the company I kept, I would also be more inclined to do shit half-assed as well.

College taught me one of my greatest life lessons, and it didn't come out of a textbook—I preferred iron-sharpens-iron friendships. It was during this time I realized how small my circle would forever be. It could be differences in culture, age, sex, race, or status (financial or academic). People who weren't encouraging me to be the best version of myself or forced themselves in my space while not pushing themselves to be better was life's way of signaling who wasn't conducive to my growth. Fred didn't work for me at the time. I didn't work for him. That's okay! It's not necessarily grounds to cut off a friendship, but I knew our relationship would have a cap. This brings me to the next set of reflection questions. While the goal of this exercise isn't to criticize anyone else's stage of life, do you have people around you who make you better? Do you feel your friends are growing alongside you or resistant to growth as a whole? Do they make you laugh when you're stressed out? Do your friends support your journey? Do they make passive-aggressive remarks that shun your decision-making? Do they share the same ambitions as you? Do they lack ambition? What are some of the general traits you see in your immediate circle of friends?

_____
_____
_____
_____
_____

I wouldn't advise you use this exercise to skim your contacts list and cut bitches off. Only you can decide whether people are in your life for a season or lifetime. However, during your college experience, a peak reflection period, if you're wondering why things aren't panning out the way you hoped, a good start would be to examine the company you're keeping. The results may shock you.

Beyond being called to do this, my passion to see this book to the end came from being tired of seeing so many of my college friends falling short in their experience, not merely because I said so, but like Fred, they reflected on their "should haves" and "could haves." While this isn't a knock on the parties, laughter, and lifelong friendships that college presents, many students are missing the opportunity to maximize the resources already embedded in their tuition fees to support in their post-undergraduate efforts.

As the earlier data reflected, forty-three percent of college grads were underemployed in their first job out of college. Of those, about two-thirds remained underemployed after five years. I believe a contributing factor to that statistic stems from the college mindset of many scholars. Just with my general observations, I found more students only fixated on the end goal of getting *out of college*, resulting in a missed opportunity to hone in on the value and tools within the journey itself. This is when I started to ask the more thought-provoking questions to my fellow scholarly colleagues.

"Have you started applying for jobs?"

"No, not yet. I'm going to start when I finish school."

"Have you spoken to someone in the career center to review your resume before you begin applying?"

"Nah, my resume is solid."

"Have you spoken to your professor to come up with a course of action to bring up your grade?"

"My professor ain't shit, and they're not checking to help me."

Although I only asked such questions when our conversation surrounded these topics, it became more apparent that many college students weren't maximizing college's tools. Despite all the resources afforded to them within the college setting to be paired with the classroom experience, many students were not taking advantage of such opportunities as the information foraging theory would denote. Many of my peers simply weren't willing to modify their strategies to maximize their academic gains.

It was never my intention to badger my friends or acquaintances about their decision-making in college. I always believed college was the safe space to forgive one another for not having it all figured out. The problem stemmed from their *expectations* not being modified to match the level of work they were putting forth to obtain those scholarly accolades and benefits. Some may call my methods judgmental. I like to believe I was being a thorough analyst. No matter what the perception was, I was ultimately inquiring about my graduating classmates' strategies with the specific intention to best tailor my approach of landing a job within my field as I inched closer to graduation. As the saying goes, "Don't be upset by the results you didn't get from the work you didn't do."

While chipping away to write this book, one morning, I woke up from an emotionally taxing and overly complex dream. My dreams always seem to be packed with intensity, just to be left with an underlying meaning that wrecks of subtlety. Sometimes I wake up, asking myself, "Damn, why did I have to go through all of that, to only end up with that $2 philosophical revelation?!" Of course, this dream left me asking the same question. However, I also believe dreams are another way God communicates with us. In a constantly changing, digitally driven world, we rarely find the time to slow down, silence our thoughts, and listen. With social media, family responsibilities, the greater demands of jobs and classes, it makes sense if we have a harder time connecting with God when met with so many distractions. The last thing we want is for Him to feel as if He is competing for our attention. I guess one of the best ways we can truly be still and know, as the popular Bible verse states, is while we're sleeping. I figured if I could wake up and remember the greatest symbols of the dream, then there was something in it worth recalling.

In my dream, I was unaware of my destination even though I had my large rolling luggage with me. I was contemplating whether I was going to get there by bus, carpool with someone else, or drive alone. I decided to drive by myself, but intentionally left my luggage elsewhere. I started to make the trek to my unknown destination. It was a gloomy day. I didn't recall any cars initially, but I was on a bridge very similar to the Golden Gate Bridge in San Francisco. As I was driving, I began to notice pockets of water on the road. It reminded me of those flood puddles that you find yourself driving through while on the freeway on a rainy day, causing the car to hydroplane. Then, water quickly started to flood the rest of the road. What started as manageable waters, quickly grew into a large aquatic wave to come crashing down on my car. The next moment, I was underwater. I acted fast to get myself out the car, even though I was still submerged. I wasn't alone for long, though. Some man, who for whatever reason seemed well-versed in going through traumatic experiences, and in my opinion was too prepared for them, swam close to me. He was signaling me on how to reach a safe space. I don't remember his face, but he seemed like a normal guy. It appeared that he dove in the water with his jeans and button-up flannel shirt. Nothing seemed supernatural about him. He just felt like a friend. While underwater, it seemed like he could have very easily grabbed me and taken me to safety. He didn't, though. He just signaled where I needed to go. Even though I was still submerged for quite some time, to my surprise when I woke up, at no point in my dream was I ever worried about dying. I knew I would live, I just had to be concerned with my *survival*. After following this man's instructions, the next thing I remember was ending up in some dark, basement-like utility closet. While in this dark space, I could recall feeling warmth like I never felt before—a source of comfort despite being in a darkened space. Although I had no idea where I was, or where I was going, I wasn't confused or panicked in the least, which is quite the contrary in my waking life. While shuffling around in the dark, I stumbled across a smaller room housing the circuit breaker. I thought that was a bit odd given that I just got my ass handed to me from water of biblical proportions to then throw electricity in the mix, but I didn't think too much into that part. While hitting the breakers, sticky notes started to illuminate around the switches, giving me clear-cut instructions on what to do next. That's when I remembered that man who initially helped me while underwater, guiding me to this very place. All these questions started to come to mind. How did this man know about this place? Has he helped someone previously get out of the same water-filled bind I was in? Did he prepare this place filled with instruction because he knew I would be confused without the notes? Like I said earlier, this man was too prepared! As the lights switched on and the sticky notes became more visible, I saw one with an arrow pointing in the direction of a door to get out of this closet. I did as the notes ordered, which led me to a busy street. Fortunately, I saw cars flying down the road, indicating life continued and I wasn't left behind after being part of some cataclysmic experience. As I started to make my way down the street on foot, I came across my former co-worker, Katrina. I shared with her what just happened to me. Despite my curiosities of wondering where the hell everyone else was while I was going through this, Katrina just listened to me speak. Katrina has always been a woman of few words, but when she talks, she most certainly has a message. She said ever so calmly, "After going through all that, whoever that man was needs to be the manager of your life." As she often does, she softly chuckled at the end of her statement and left me alone with something to think about. I woke up from my dream. The more I reflected on it, the more I began to smile. There were three primary symbols that stood out to me. You've probably already figured one or two of them out. For the sake of ensuring no reader is confused, I'll elaborate.

The first symbol in my dream was the luggage. I knew my luggage represented personal baggage—preventing me from moving toward my destination. It was just weighing me down. I still didn't know where I was going, but I respected that the luggage could not come with me. Then, despite having transportation options, I was compelled to drive alone. Sometimes people around you don't understand why you have to disconnect and go on a journey as a lone ranger. I knew I needed to, though. My dream was the premise of this entire chapter *even before I was done writing it!* We are not meant to ride the same wavelength as everyone else. We sometimes have to isolate ourselves and proceed differently than the norm to see maximized results. Even from the framework of education, all your friends can't come with you on your journey. Your entire family cannot come with you on *your* journey! There will be times where you are meant to go somewhere by yourself because being alone is easier than having to constantly justify to people your reasons for doing things they will never understand. Simply put, your journey wasn't designed for anyone else but you to be there. Your friends may not understand why you spend all your time in the career center. Your family may not understand why you are so "wound up from being in your books too long." Your significant other may not understand why you called it quits, because you started to realize how insignificant and handicapping they were to your educational, professional, mental, emotional, and spiritual growth. It wasn't until I woke up and reflected on my dream, that I truly understood how my journey just wasn't meant for everyone to tag along.

The second symbol that stood out to me was that ultimate doomsday prepper dude. That man who showed up out of nowhere, if you haven't guessed it already, was God. He was a friend to me in that moment when no one and nothing else was around. I trusted the man in the dreams because I didn't have another choice. He didn't have this weird authoritative hold on me that many non-believers love to unreasonably attach to God. He was just present. Like my dream, our lives are filled with chaotic experiences, unsure of where we're going or what we're doing, but He was present. My journey was filled with uneasiness, uncertainty, and I'm sure, after the potential of drowning, I was exhausted. Even with that, He was still present.

The third takeaway from my dream was God's actions in it. He didn't just swoop in and save me. Yes, He guided me underwater, and even left sticky notes in the utility closet, but He still let me struggle. When I woke up, I started to ask myself why? Then it hit me. In this dream, God didn't come back later on, looking to collect for saving my life. All He wanted was for me to be an *active participant in furthering myself*. I find it to be no mere coincidence that I would get this revelation in the midst of writing this chapter ironically titled, Don't Half-Ass Shit. It was still up to me to take the necessary measures to figure out what He wanted me to do next. He wanted me to remain diligent and vigilant in my life, so that I could fulfill His purpose. Considering this is key as a soon-to-be graduate, which is why I pose these questions to you:

- What more can you do to remain diligent and vigilant in your tasks to land a job within your field while still enrolled in college?
- How do you intend on maintaining these habits?
- What will you do when people begin to criticize you on matters they don't understand?
- How will you react?
- What can you do differently today, to make the difference tomorrow?
- As always, feel free to grab more paper, if necessary.

_____
_____
_____
_____

I know all of this seems easier said than done, and trust me, it is. If I didn't understand how complex these notions were, I wouldn't have given you an entire book on them. These concepts require you to give your all in your physical actions and spiritual ones. It's one thing to give your all and be disappointed, but it's another to complain about why life didn't turn out the way you wanted because of work you didn't put enough into. This reminds me of a passage I came across in a devotional by Kesha Trippett. It was titled, *God Rewards Diligence*. Surely enough, the reading shared some overlap with the theme of this chapter. She used the example of Suzanne starting a job and having difficulties with learning her new role, leading to discouragement and hesitation about her career field. Despite Suzanne's challenges, she recognized the importance of thoroughly doing her part to maximize her results.

> There are many people like Suzanne who are having trouble seeing and seizing God's promotions in front of them, because they didn't expect it to be so difficult to obtain. Just because you're being challenged doesn't mean you're not where you're supposed to be. And just because everything seems easy doesn't mean you are where you're supposed to be. Grace is not the absence of great effort. **Grace works alongside our great effort and it creates something amazing!**

Diligence requires we do things differently than our average college counterparts, like occasionally turning down those campus functions to apply for jobs and internships. Diligence is about making a conscious decision to actively apply ourselves so that our mark on the world will be a lasting one. God rewards diligence.

Trippett concluded the passage with this prayer, which I also felt fitting to bring the chapter to a close:

Father God, I thank you for your wisdom. Help me to focus on the goal instead of the challenges. Strengthen me, Lord. Help me learn from my mistakes and get better and better each day. I choose not to operate with a lazy mind or a slack hand. Help me to be a diligent soul that is diligent in every area of my life. From my relationships and family, to my workplace, to my spiritual walk with you, to my finances and everything else, help me do what I need to do. Help me receive your grace and apply your wisdom in my life. In Jesus' name, Amen.

Chapter 4

Reset and Rejuvenate Your Mindset

What more can you possibly do to ensure you land a job within your field after college? I repeated this question all throughout undergrad. This can be daunting to think about, especially if you're already burnt out from the higher education setting. However, this question was necessary as I narrowed down some strategies that best supported my endeavors post-undergrad. These concepts may seem obvious for some, while others may dismiss these behaviors as "basic" and fail to realize the far deeper meaning that such actions have on one's personal and professional development. It's ultimately up to you to examine your current situation and determine how you'll effectively integrate, modify, or maintain these methods in your life. It won't be a walk in the park by any stretch of the imagination. However, the best outcomes usually result from a decisionmaker considering the long-term effects of their present actions. What you're doing now will determine how smooth your transition will be after undergrad. This is a time to develop a trait which surprisingly so few people obtain—accountability. It's in these moments students either rise to the occasion or push every excuse in the book as to why they are not adhering to their full potential. Being "too tired" or "exhausted" is common. It also doesn't help when the demands of life always feel more enhanced when trying to pursue your degree. However, the way you navigate these periods of sluggishness, while keeping your eye on the end goal of completing your degree, can make or break your college experience. To best tackle college, it helps to identify the factors you're juggling while enrolled. Write out the factors in your life that are exhausting you.

Culturally and socially, we've created an unfair notion that the youth *can't* and *shouldn't* be exhausted. Personally speaking, being raised in a black household, we know this all too well because we're often met with remarks such as, "What the hell are you tired from? You don't work a full-time job." When we're not defending our work ethic in the home or socially, baby boomers are harping on how lazy the youth is, unfairly measuring their work conditions long ago to those of the younger generation without consideration of additional variables that keep such a comparison in the gray area. It's also not conducive for students to enter higher education with a clean mental slate. This was my case. I hadn't yet walked on college ground and already felt that I didn't have the breathing room to decompress from high school, let alone take on the newfound challenges of a university.

After graduating high school, I was drained. Although eager to start a new chapter in my life, not only was exhaustion prevalent from the education system and society as a whole, but as a budding teenager who naturally yearned for more independence from my mom. Most teens want this, but it was especially important for my mental health and our relationship. This was the first step to reset my mindset. I viewed my relationship with my mom for what it was, acknowledging that space was the best anecdote. College gave me that and I took it.

Despite my mother and me having differences, we still had to come together at times to navigate the financials of attending school when filling out the financial aid application. Other than that, I was on my own, and she always reminded me of it too. As a first-generation college student, she helped where she could, but I was solely responsible for overseeing my entire college career and the monies associated with it. My mom wasn't the parent who would call the school to oversee their student's financials. It's not because she didn't care, but because she simply didn't know how. Like many college students, the financial particulars of attending school put a strain on me, even with financial aid. Since I worked in the cashier's office as a student assistant, it was impossible to be oblivious about the actual cost of attendance. Seeing delinquent student accounts daily and talking to a plethora of parents calling on behalf of their kids who had no clue or care about handling their own financial records, made me adamant about getting my money's worth. This was the motivation I needed to find strategies to best pace myself in this academic marathon, despite always being on the cusp of a mental breakdown. I wanted to be well-versed in as many academic regards as possible, because by not doing so, I wouldn't have gained the necessary tools to best rejuvenate myself at times of burn out.

Within weeks of establishing my routine in college, the varying wavelengths of student behavior became more apparent. You've got the overachievers, underachievers, and those who rode the in-between. Collectively, all of these academic personalities played a part in why I wrote this book in the first place. The groundwork you lay to obtain the degree is just as important as the diploma itself. While many of my peers were fixed on just getting the hell out of school, if anything, I was nervous as I continued to inch toward graduation! I was constantly met with competing perceptions from people who felt the education system was a sham ideology. Those are the ones who easily list all the big names who didn't attend college and became successful. While I respected their position, I was confident education was the route for me. Naturally, these comments still invoked a sense of self-doubt since I didn't want to be part of the statistic working outside of my degree just because I took the first job that was offered to me upon graduating. That alone, was enough to ensure I had some guarantees when I graduated. I didn't want my damn time to be wasted!

Whatever your motivation is for seeing your degree to the end is what's needed in those moments of sluggishness that no one is exempt from. Your motivations may change with time, but finding your "center" in the midst of the chaos is vital to best reset your mindset as you pursue your degree.

Now consider this. What was one of your first defining moments which prompted you to attend school in the first place? What is/was a defining moment or factor to motivate you to continue your education? Your response should be kept close to always reference. Use it as a gentle reminder to keep going.

_____
_____
_____
_____
_____

_____
_____
_____
_____

Chapter 5

Develop and Maintain Strong Classroom Practices

What more can you do on campus and in the classroom to better prepare for what's to come after completing your degree? Is there anything more you can do that won't crowd your plate? No matter if you are attending a community college or a world-renowned university, if you want a degree-specific job as soon as you graduate, mere class attendance is not going to cut it, even if you are a straight-A student.

Like anything worth having, you get out of it, what you put in. College is no exception, starting with classroom practices. It doesn't matter if a class is highly engaging or ever so dull. Attending class regularly is vital for your overall academic investment. Your tuition is what's paying the salaries of your professors. If school was a brick and mortar business like Target, for example, once you've paid for a service or product, there would be an unquestionable expectation to receive goods in exchange. Why isn't the same holding true for your attendance?

Your investment in education isn't just in the form of tuition. There is also an investment of time and participation while in class. This means coming to class and staying the entire duration to truly get your money's worth. You're paying to be there whether you are sitting in that cold-ass tiny metal seat or not. I'll be damned if I went to a steakhouse and paid for the most expensive thing on the menu, just to walk out without eating. Students should feel the same way about going to class! Call me cheap, frugal, or goodie two shoes. I really don't care. My grind in school boiled down to this—I refused to waste my money.

In what world is it okay to pay full price for something and negatively discount yourself at the same time? That's what I saw so many students doing, not even realizing it when they chose not to put their best foot forward in the classroom. When in class, ask questions. You're paying to have them answered. Engage in classroom discussions. You're paying for professional development as you interact with people with differing viewpoints than yours. Make this experience work for you and your finances. Your classroom attendance comes with making a conscious decision to not fall distracted to applications on your laptop or checking your phone every few minutes. Although difficult in the growing digital age, these practices go beyond being a star pupil. It's about making sure you aren't missing out on what you rightfully paid for.

Had you been in talks for a lucrative deal that was personally beneficial, I'm sure you would comb through every intricate detail to ensure you didn't miss anything. Absolutely nothing would distract you from seeing this deal come to pass. The same holds true when actively committing to the classroom experience for your degree. Cashing in on the college experience means submitting your best work, even if it's just a draft, so you can receive the best feedback to further develop your analytical, written, and oral communication skills. Don't simply turn in bullshit just to say you submitted something before the deadline. I'll repeat that for the people in the back. *Don't simply turn in bullshit just to say you submitted something before the deadline!* That is equally wasted time for both you and your professor, since you are paying for their feedback!

Tackling Office Hours

Another issue many college students have is the misguided understanding of a professor's office hours. As an adjunct faculty member, I speak from experience when I say many college professors feel underutilized. Naturally, students who need additional assistance use office hours. That's what it's for. However, rather than this being a time of *supplemental* support, at times, it quickly turns into an uncomfortable plea bargain for extra credit from students who didn't genuinely apply themselves initially—half-assed. This isn't to say that "good" students don't go in and ask for extra credit, but it is a missed opportunity to maximize your resources. As I've seen time and time again, faculty members are not inclined to genuinely support a student who approaches them at the eleventh hour, especially when they've been readily available to assist well before crunch time. Teachers are not in the business of showing favor to students who hope a few assignments will result in a passing grade after poorly contributing all semester. Office hours are to gain additional understanding, not a substitute session after not attending class without a previously approved agreement between you and the professor. These meetings are not reserved for students to obtain a copy of the lecture notes because they weren't paying attention in class. Office hours are meant to be *coupled* with your classroom experience. If you have additional questions that class time didn't permit you to ask, that would be the place to get your answers. Coming prepared with materials that are specifically confusing to you is what office hours are for. Gaining additional feedback and coaching as you work toward your midterm and final projects is what office hours are reserved for.

When continuing to frame these examples from the lens of business, think of office hours as an extended warranty on a product you purchased. We'll use a washing machine, for example. If you didn't purchase a washing machine, you wouldn't see the value of buying the optional warranty attached to the purchase of that washing machine. After purchasing the washing machine, it starts to malfunction. If you have exhausted every possibility to fix that washing machine by yourself and are still having trouble, at least now you can better articulate your trial and error to the warranty company. Since you've covered all your bases, the warranty coverage allows you to obtain additional support so the service provider doesn't waste their time repeating steps of what you've already done. The same goes for the classroom setting and office hours. Office hours (warranty) hold no weight if your contributions to the classroom were subpar.

Get Selfish about Your Education

Just as much as students experience burnout, teachers are subject to the same sluggishness. My former high school teacher, we'll call them Teacher M, later decided to change careers. When I asked their reasoning for doing so they replied, "I got tired of teaching kids who didn't want to learn or care." Teacher M always strived to find innovative ways to relay new information. Unfortunately, it didn't mean much if their efforts weren't appreciated or reciprocated. Students often don't consider how their efforts or lack thereof become determining factors in why instructors' lights become dimmed—impacting the quality of education for the greater student population. Whether it be showing up late to class just because, leaving early, and not participating in class discussions, that can negatively impact an individual who is just trying to do their job. It boils down to courtesy and respect for the classroom. Above anything, as a student, you owe it to yourself to be present in every aspect of the word to maximize your dollar. This rejuvenates teachers to continue to educate students who have a desire to learn, while further encouraging them to go above the call of duty to support scholars by any means. Many of my teachers are still my mentors, points of contact for letters of recommendation, and references for job opportunities. I obtained phenomenal academic support as a direct result of proving myself to them in the classroom! These relationships propelled me professionally and have been invaluable since graduating. College was the time for me to get selfish about what I wanted long-term and pull on every resource possible to get it.

We live in a world that's quick to shun us for thinking about ourselves. Even when exercising a healthy degree of selfishness, we're met with greater ridicule from people who no longer benefit from our inability to practice self-care. If the goal is to be successful after college, you must make yourself a priority while enrolled. Ms. Kim, my mama away from home, would always tell me, "It's about you. This is your time to be selfish." She took the stigma out of being everything to everybody and reminded me to use college as my launching pad. I couldn't achieve what I hoped for had I not taken full advantage of the opportunities around me, regardless of what anyone said. Too much money and time is at stake for you not to be selfish. You *should* be expecting a payoff after you completed your degree. You *should* have multiple job offers. By not taking advantage of the resources college affords you to be a success, when it's all said and done, you merely become another student gypped by the education system, dumping thousands of dollars into an institution for a piece of paper you may not even use. That doesn't have to be your reality. The responsibility to change that notion is up to you.

Chapter 6

Internships

Being in Los Angeles and having an interest in television news, I applied for tons of opportunities. Since L.A. is the number two television market behind New York City and still holds the skewed view that all of California is Hollywood, a land filled with opportunity, that translated into loads of competition from all across the world. This made obtaining an internship that much harder.

When speaking with friends of other local schools who were interning left and right, I realized many of them attended USC or UCLA. After speaking with them a bit more, they said their campus resources were the primary reason they were afforded the opportunity to at least get an interview. Many of my friends said their campus resources were far more abundant just by way of going to a big named institution. While my non-Cal State LA friends most certainly deserved every opportunity they were granted, I also made the correlation that many big named employers were partnering with bigger named institutions like the USCs and UCLAs, leaving an even smaller chance for me to land an impressive internship of my own. While my school resources weren't poor, I knew I had to work harder to differentiate myself to be considered for opportunities, regardless if I brought the same quality *or better* work than my counterparts from more notable institutions. Not every student will attend an ivy league or a world-renowned university, but it doesn't negate the fact that those students are just as valuable and have something equally phenomenal to offer. This forced me to be more resilient and resourceful in obtaining my broadcast and communication-based opportunities.

While many college students obtain internships, a lot of students are going about them the wrong way. Internships are an opportunity to gain valuable real-world experience outside of the classroom. This is a time to better understand your interest and dislikes as you're determining your career path. It's also a great opportunity to see how some of the concepts you are learning in the classroom apply to a specific setting. Internships act as a much-needed eye-opener to either reinforce what you *thought* your passion was or debunk your ideologies of your major altogether.

Since I was interested in the communications and broadcast journalism sector, specifically television, I was initially instructed to just obtain any broadcast internship to get my foot in the door. As I started applying for internships, all of which I sought outside of university assistance, I got my first opportunity at a radio station. Although radio was not my long-term interest, I used the internship to gain valuable experience and make viable contacts that further assisted in my journey down the line.

Don't Wait. It May Be Too Late.

The first order of business when seeking internships is not to wait until the last minute to obtain one. When I was in school, I started applying for internships my junior year of college. Getting an internship as a junior also comes with the added bonus of giving yourself time to obtain more than one opportunity for the duration of your college career. For many students, the beginning of junior year is an ideal time to at least browse internships. This is because internship credit opportunities are typically reserved for upperclassman depending on your major and school of attendance. When I started searching for opportunities, I didn't feel a sense of obligation to go out and get just any internship for the sake of having something on my resume before graduating. This window of time gave me the breathing room to be strategic in how I utilized my time to gain experience outside of the classroom.

Although rare, some scholars attempt to land an internship *after* they graduate with the hopes it will help them better land a job. While I think this is still worth a try if a student hasn't obtained one before graduating, keep in mind that many employers reserve internships for currently enrolled students. Some opportunities even require a student to be enrolled full-time. It's overwhelming at times to juggle an internship with a full course load, but time management and organizational skills can help students keep it all together. Take measures to reevaluate your schedule with your guidance counselor or academic advisor, express your goals, and pull on their insight to come up with a course of action that is academically sustainable. It's counterproductive to take on an internship for the mere sake of saying you had one if you don't actively adjust your schedule to mentally connect to the experience.

When considering an internship, ask yourself, what are you hoping to learn that you couldn't within the classroom? This will help tailor your internship search to ensure the opportunity enhances your skills in your respective industry. This question also holds you accountable to not get an internship for course credit just to have it on your resume before graduating. Companies can quickly decipher which students are hungry for the opportunity or just there to take up space for a measly two credit boost on their transcript. The dead giveaway is when a student shows up to the office with the same half-assed energy they gave in class.

Um. Am I Getting Paid for This?

The next thing to consider is payment—the elephant in the room. When internship searching, you'll find that many of them are unpaid. A lot organizations that don't pay interns will often offer course credit. Some organizations may offer both. If you come across an "opportunity" that doesn't offer either, run for the hills! This may be the greatest indicator the business isn't all that viable. Organizations have to be recognized as a business for the college to appropriately honor course credit. Anything beyond that is just a volunteer opportunity, or a slimy way for janky businesses to abuse the time and resources of college students. Under that same token though, some legitimately recognized organizations will pull the same stunt. That's why it's imperative when doing your research to thoroughly vet the business, just as you would an actual job.

Sometimes, as college students, the eagerness to obtain an opportunity for the sake of building a resume kicks in, leaving you falling under the spell that the organization is doing *you* a favor by taking you on as an intern. This may cause you to overlook some of the red flags associated with that business because you're desperate to launch your career. Organizations can see that, and some will go as far as playing on those emotions to deplete you of your resources—the long distance you travel by public transportation, burning loads of gas for an unpaid internship as a broke college student, using your personal computer to handle company affairs, or restlessly working for them at odd hours. All of these scenarios, I've either witnessed or gone through personally. While the opportunity is appreciated, never forget that your service, time, and energy is just as valuable to them as gaining experience is to you, no matter how out of touch some of them come across. More importantly, your time, energy, and invested resources are important to you. You should consider them as such when seeking internships that are in best alignment with the vision for yourself and your current routine.

Defining Your Ethics as a Budding Professional

Interning is also a great starting point to better identify what you stand for as a budding professional. While I respected the totem pole with regards to biting my tongue on matters I didn't necessarily agree with, I became better in tune with my positionality about certain business practices. Along my internship journey, I came across my fair share of kind, rude, and flat-out arrogant people. In my case, I found that the nicer individuals were often the better workers, while the ornery ones half-assed their responsibilities. Of course, I got stuck "learning" underneath some of the unpleasant seeds; but it made me more conscious of my actions and attitude. I started making promises to myself that as I grew as a professional, I would not treat others with the same piss-poor regard that I got. After encountering blatant disrespect from "professionals" who felt they could behave in such a manner because I was just a measly intern, coupled with being unpaid, lent greater reason for me to become more intentional with how I was expelling my time and energy—even at the college level. Despite all that I went through, my takeaways from the experiences were far more valuable than the chaos.

Internships Are Primarily for Learning, Not Job Seeking.

The most exceptional benefit of interning is that it affords you with great networking opportunities (we will discuss more in the next chapter). Your internship can spark potential business endeavors later on in your career. These opportunities act as a platform to showcase your skills to people already in the business. Although normal to hope for that "breakout moment" for someone to take you under their wing and open up additional doors, remember, you are supposed to open your own doors, not take solace in the opportunities you think someone else can grant you. With that, never go into an internship with the *expectation* of getting a job afterward. Go into your internship to gain experience *only*. You are there to learn. Trust that your hard work will shine through just because you enjoy the process of doing it. Anything else produced from that internship is a bonus.

Know When to Move On

I ran into a lot of people who were waiting around at internships. I noticed some interns, some of whom were no longer in school, stayed at these organizations with hopes the company was going to give them their big break. While possible, this is still a gamble and can hinder you from exploring other opportunities that can lead to a position after college.

It wasn't all bad though. If anything, after speaking with my internship counterparts, many of them said the opportunity rescued them. Even without payment, the internship consistently gave them something productive to do and a safe space to explore their creativity in this dog-eat-dog world. However, many of them didn't know when to take that leap of faith and move on.

In your gut, you know when your growth has been stumped. Don't ignore that feeling. One of the worst things anyone can do to is to stay at an organization just going through the motions, entrapping themselves in the possibility of something better coming out of that one opportunity. By doing this, you ultimately remain stagnant and fail to explore the experiences in the world that were waiting on you all along. You just had to leap. Internships are no exception.

Students, be very wary of companies that are *okay* with keeping you around without a tentative internship end time or promises of a promotion of sorts without any proof to show for it. Real internships typically have a designated start and end time. This is typically determined by the company and properly coordinated with the college to ensure students receive course credit. If you negotiate with that company to stay onboard for a paid position, especially after dedicating time as an unpaid intern, so be it. On the other hand, trust me when I say, you do more self-harm by staying with a company you are not growing at while they dangle a "possible" job opportunity over your head. These organizations may just be looking for free labor. Even if this isn't specific to your case, trust your instincts when it's time to move on. After all, you took this internship to learn and *move on*. Like all good things… or bad, they must come to an end. The standard of only obtaining one internship while enrolled in college is bogus. Explore as many additional opportunities as possible. Just make sure your internships are intentional, and not merely to meet a quota.

While interning at the radio station, I was hardworking and had an eagerness to learn without any ulterior motive. That allowed me to establish phenomenal relationships in the most organic form, despite realizing my time there had an expiration date. God had placed it on my heart to go after something bigger and better, and that's exactly what I sought out. Despite venturing off for other endeavors, I left on wonderful terms, connecting with people from all the departments—sales, promotions, street team, and with on-air talent. I was still contacted by the station to participate in additional events beyond my internship. It was evident to me that I had shown them a piece of what I could do, personally and professionally. Leaving was only a technicality. And hey, if an opportunity for their company came up that I might be a good fit for, they would know how to reach me, if I was still available. I didn't need to stay around to be in their face all the time to prove myself. I trusted my endeavors beyond the radio station would do that, all while building a more notable resume.

As my radio internship came to an end, the internship coordinator filled out the corresponding paperwork to submit to my school for course credit. As I sat down with him one last time, I reiterated my gratefulness for my first broadcast opportunity. Of course, I was a bit emotional. The coordinator, who I always perceived to be this stern guy with this silent dominance throughout my internship, looked at me a little differently than before. For the first time, he looked at me like a proud dad and said, "Alexis, you came here to leave." I swiftly wiped my eyes with tissues, overwhelmed with appreciation, recognizing that his words entailed so much more. It was his way of also saying, he too, saw bigger and better opportunities for me, and this internship was only a small stop along my journey.

When you stand in your truth that you have more to learn and are willing to obtain that knowledge by any means necessary, something will click on the inside of you. It doesn't matter if you stay or leave that organization. If you maintain strong networking skills, trust that your impact was a lasting one. If you believe you made your mark, maintaining communication with these contacts is the breeding grounds to potentially work with them again on a future project, or even full-time for an opportunity beyond internship status.

When I walked out the station's doors, I had this newfound energy to keep applying for TV news internships. Although it seemed as if everything happened in beautiful succession looking back, I still experienced doubt and had to take detours to get me where I was going. Of course, life quickly rained on my parade. After doing as instructed to obtain any broadcast experience, it seemed like the finish line was constantly moving. Now I was being told that my radio internship didn't make me a strong enough applicant for television opportunities. I was applying for small news outlets, and major news stations such as ABC and NBCUniversal. I even worked at Disneyland for a bit, making a far ass commute with hopes that by being a part of the Walt Disney Company, I would have the leverage to get in at ABC. I didn't. I changed gears and applied for NBCUniversal multiple times for various positions. I even interviewed often, and still never got an internship, which makes me laugh now because I ended up producing and anchoring for an NBC News affiliate in Oregon after graduating.

Although extremely bothered by the sense of rejection and feeling as if I wasn't being afforded the necessary opportunity to launch my career, I couldn't dwell on being told "no." I kept reminding myself I was still in college, so the pressure wasn't as great to hurry up and figure out my next move. I was still taking full-time units so there was plenty of work to keep busy. Tapping into that same source of determination to pursue my education and gain valuable experience, I ended up attaining my second internship with a boutique PR firm a few months after, which also afforded me course credit for my communication degree. This internship was great because it revealed that the public relations aspect of communication is not my favorite line of work. Despite taking a temporary detour from my broadcast focus, I remained intentional in gaining internship experience consistent with my majors, paying close attention to how these opportunities were interconnected to how my life would unfold.

Chapter 7

Networking

While I was in college, I attended an assortment of leadership conferences. One conference in particular, resonated with me the most. I met other over-achieving students and listened to guest speakers talk about their success. Two pieces of wisdom came out of that conference which have stuck with me to this very day. One of the speakers said, "*Networking* is the one letter difference between *not working*." Wow. Powerful, right? That's what I thought too. The other jewel that would clip to my spirit for a lifetime was what the CEO of the foundation's conference echoed every session. He said, "It's not about what you know. It's not even about who you know, but about who knows you." These two statements became the premise of my changed outlook when it came to landing a job after college.

If I wanted to make the most out of this degree, it would require far more work than blindly applying for jobs with hopes I would hear back in a timely manner. As I said earlier, you can't walk across the stage and expect a job offer simply because *you have arrived*. I can personally attest to many of my opportunities manifesting by way of having the necessary tools to *sell myself*, as I viewed every encounter as a chance to network. It was by interning at the radio station that I networked with my now good friend DeMira, who pulled strings to get me another internship opportunity at BET Networks. It was By viewing my college professors as more than just teachers, I could better see the benefit of maintaining those relationships as resources for insight into job opportunities and further connections in my field of study. One of my professors afforded me the information to connect with (and mildly harass) a former Cal State LA alum and Producer at KTLA 5 News. That producer then pulled strings to get me an internship there at the cusp of them relaunching their internship program after not having one for some time. I'll talk about this opportunity from a spiritual standpoint later in the book, but at this point, pay attention to the significance in making yourself known beyond the resume. These practices can unlock future opportunities when it comes to your career and success. You will no longer operate in the mindset of *if*.

"If I get this internship, they will hire me after."

"If I pass these classes this semester, I will start looking for internships."

"If I had come from a wealthy family, my connections would be better."

Enough.

While "if" mentalities aren't a bad thing, and can give us something nice to think about, many of us get locked into only the "if." *If* statements can act as a crutch to prevent you from taking matters into your own hands to further your reach and manifest your own destiny. Turn your "if" into "when." You are reclaiming your power and will no longer play Russian Roulette with your opportunities after college. This comes with actively letting everyone know who you are and what your intentions are long-term. Some of my comments to myself when climbing through the ranks were, "When I finish undergrad, I am going straight to grad school." "When I am in undergrad, I will not wait until the last minute to get an internship." "When I get internship opportunities, my goal is to let my work speak for itself. I will not be concerned with a potential job offer following my internship. I will be present in the moment to learn and retain the necessary skills for the future." I found that by verbalizing my "when" statements, I held myself accountable to do everything within reason to make those opportunities happen.

Reframing my thinking and language also made it easier to market myself when I was networking. I found the more confident I portrayed myself to be, the more confidence other networkers had in me to be a solid addition to any company that I worked with. It was, and always will be, essential for me to be my greatest advocate, especially while networking. Networking determined if people would remember or forget me. Those encounters determine if people would speak highly of me in rooms that I'm not even in, for opportunities that I didn't even know were out there. Strong networking skills determine if your professional connections are just temporary or lifelong.

To this day, I still have connections at every place I worked. This affords me the corporate wonder of the world—access. I have access to conversation, insight, mentorship, job opportunities, extended connections, and more, whenever I so chose. As long as I continued to develop within my respective career so that the professional relationship could remain mutually beneficial, I immediately increased my chances of gaining employment soon after graduating.

What's in Your Toolbox?

What are some tools to best network? I have three: mastery of your elevator pitch, business cards, and an ever-growing networking spreadsheet. In that exact order! To be most successful in your job search after undergrad comes with knowing how to sell yourself. An elevator pitch is essentially your professional interest and background in a thirty-second or less nutshell. The phrase "elevator pitch" comes from the made-up scenario, yet likely chance, that if you happened to be in an elevator with someone who could unlock opportunities for you, especially within your field, you can tell them why they should keep you on their radar. For example, if you're a film student and aspire to be a Hollywood movie director and happen to be in the elevator with Steven Spielberg, it would be the hope that you one, don't pass up the opportunity to tell him who you are, and two, aren't tongue-tied when you do so. With that, the best elevator pitches are those that are practiced—but not over-rehearsed—and concise, yet organic in your delivery.

Some people may write me off here because they think delivering an elevator pitch is easier for someone like myself who majored in communication. While there may be some truth to that statement, knowing how to sell yourself and professionally communicate that *you are the shit*, is required in any industry. When thinking about your elevator pitch, consider key points about yourself, something memorable, your educational background, your life circumstances that guided you to that career, and anything else you deem valuable for people to know when considering you. This isn't the time to show humility. This is your opportunity to professionally brag about yourself. When it's time to give your spiel, stand with confidence and speak with conviction to emphasize that you are a force to be reckoned with. My first elevator pitch while in undergrad went a little something like this:

My name is Alexis Thrower. I am a third-year at Cal State LA, double-majoring in communication and television, film, and media studies with an option in journalism. Public speaking has always come natural to me and I have consistently developed the skill since I was a kid; which is why I intend on pursuing my master's degree in communication following my undergraduate program. I would like to work as a news anchor and reporter, while also exploring other communication-based endeavors that allow me to work in sectors that I am passionate about, such as media and education. I am currently open to internship and mentorship opportunities that will afford me with the necessary experience to further myself within my respective career. I would love to speak with you further to better understand how you have come to the position you are currently in. Any insight you could provide would be appreciated.

These elevator pitches unlock the door to continue dialogue with potential employers, associates, or future business partners. Without one, communication either won't happen at all or will grow stagnant, very quickly. Don't think for one second I didn't use my elevator pitch to help get my internship at KTLA or when meeting DeMira for the first time to help me land my opportunity with BET, in addition to handing her my business card (which I will get to in a second).

As an additional note, when considering your elevator pitch, remember that these statements are fluid. As you continue to better yourself and your circumstances, your elevator pitch should be indicative of your current situation. When I initially started grad school, I was also beginning my career as a full-time journalist. As I continued to hone in on my interests, I made sure my pitch was consistent with that. With just a few minor adjustments, my newer pitch went something like this:

My name is Alexis Thrower. I'm currently pursuing my master's degree in communication from Johns Hopkins with a dual-emphasis in public and media relations and health communication. In addition to my master's degree, in undergrad, I double-majored in communications and television, film, and media studies with an option in journalism. Hence, my current line of work as a news anchor and producer for a local television station in Eugene, Oregon. My career interests and goals are to continue within the communications and journalistic sector, while also adhering to my passion for education, as I have always loved and appreciated the classroom setting and serving others. I want to take my experience and implement it back into the classroom as a college instructor in the areas of communication and journalism. If you know of any opportunities that you think I may be a good fit for, I would love to speak with you further, and maybe even connect over coffee.

Side bar—I don't even like coffee, but you catch what I'm throwing. Your elevator pitch gives you a solid foundation to work from when it comes to exchanging contact information in a situation that would have otherwise, been a missed opportunity.

Now that you have some background information on what it means to give a solid elevator pitch, it's your turn. With the space provided, I want you to think about your dream job or opportunity. Imagine yourself with any person who you believe could help take your career to the next level. How would you sell yourself? What would you say if you only had thirty seconds with them in the elevator? You've got to make a lasting impression. Remember, don't be afraid to boast about yourself. This is your time. You don't have any of it to waste since you want a job immediately after college. Go!

_____

_____

_____

After you've developed a strong elevator pitch, it's time to think about your business card. Whether you're at a networking event, or just out and about, you must have business cards on deck. I understand this may be a foreign concept to many college students, but cards still make a statement. It says you mean business and want to be taken seriously. Business cards are a part of your brand. Believe it or not, you started developing a brand long before you started applying for jobs. Business cards are a way to leave a piece of yourself with someone. When you come in contact with people, not only will you obtain their information for follow-up, but business cards provide something tangible for people to remember you by. After delivering a solid elevator pitch, and leaving them with your business card, you immediately strengthen your chances to be burned into the individual's memory, which is equivalent to hitting the jackpot while in the market for jobs.

You may be asking yourself, "I'm in college so what would I even put on my business cards?" Great question, my friend! Your business cards don't have to be super fancy. The basics include your name, methods of contact, university of attendance, major, and maybe a link to your work and social media handles. You can even add your specific career interests, so if someone happens to hear of opportunities, they'll recall your interest via the business card and may further connect you with the hiring manager, for example. In my case, I took what some workforce professionals deemed a "risk" on my business card by having my picture on it. My thought process was that I was going to probably use my face for whatever job I was going after, especially in the broadcast industry. My image was just as vital to my brand as my work, and my business card was going to reflect that.

As a side note, please get rid of any unprofessional emails. Please. No hotsugamomma26@bootylicious.com or nicepecksmark@superbuff.net. If you've got something similar to that or a distracting email of sorts, *throw the whole email address away!* If your business cards are aids for you to leave a lasting impression, you don't want potential employers to be left with that, as an unprofessional email address can overshadow the great qualities you have to offer. You also don't want to make the professional exchange awkward if you have a risqué email address that people must use to contact you. Although this seems like an obvious concept, you'd be surprised how many people miss the mark on this. If you doubt your email is professional, then it's safe to say you probably need another one.

Some people believe business cards are dated with the rise of the digital age. While I'm not here to knock on the wonders that technology has afforded us, "old-fashioned" is sometimes the most refreshing facet in the workforce, especially for recruiters. As I mentioned earlier, business cards leave a personal piece of you with the individual and physically creates a distinction in the everyday processes that we perform on our electronic devices. This is especially true when entering someone's details in our contacts list. We've all done it; quickly exchanged information with someone and stored them as a new contact in our phones just to fail to recall their name a few days later. Unless you're like our sacred old folks who only have a whopping seven contacts in their phone, the majority of the world is left scrolling through contacts like dumbasses hoping to recall the name of who we networked with, knowing full well we have no clue if we're looking for Craig or Day-Day. But, if you hand someone a business card, and God forbid you be a young person using this classic method, now you've become an instant rarity and a name worth remembering.

Keep in mind, networking is not strictly confined to mixers, but anywhere you step foot. With that, you never want to be without business cards. I remember ordering five hundred cards and keeping an entire box in my car. This also helped tremendously since I was a young woman who constantly changed bags. I was able to put business cards in every purse to ensure I never went without.

While processing these tactics to become a better networker, here's some food for thought. Whether you are at a professional mixer or simply out and about—don't restrict your communications to people solely in your industry. Never underestimate Gary the garbage man. Networking is a two-way street. It's not only about what a person can do for you. Think of networking as an interconnected web, in which you have connections and they have connections. They may not have the support within their industry to support you directly, but may know someone who can, and vice versa. Your immediate instinct may be to write off Gary as someone who can't help you since you're not interested in the sanitation business, but you have no clue who Gary has in his contacts list. You may be a budding journalist, and Gary's daughter is an executive producer for a TV station looking for new talent. Gary may very well be the owner of the garbage company and can teach you a thing or two about entrepreneurship. This goes back to one of the initial phrases I started this chapter with. "It's not what you know. It's not even about who you know, but about who knows you." Gary the garbage man may not tell you who he knows. However, if you give him your business card, you never know what could come from that exchange. Never miss an opportunity to tell people who the hell you are! When networking, discounting anyone is a disservice to your ultimate goal—to get the job in your field.

Even if you are making connections left and right by implementing these strategies for success, when networking, don't assume everyone else is up to par with these professional practices. You will meet tons of people who don't have business cards and may not understand your reason for still using this method, but that's none of their business, unless you care to get technical with them. If you find that person to be a viable resource in whatever industry they may be in and they don't have a business card, then, of course, I advise you to pull out your phone, plug them in as a contact or place them in the notes section of your smart device. Once an introduction has been made, give your elevator pitch, spark some conversation, and exchange contact information digitally or with business cards.

Now on to the third networking practice, which is understanding the value of follow-up. When you're attending networking events or just meeting people casually, not only are you looking to give out your business card, but also seeking to add professional contacts to your roster. If you're like me, and have a poor memory, or have a mind that races a million miles a minute, as soon as you get a free moment, while it's still fresh in your brain, break away from the scene and jot down a few memorable points from your conversation on the back of their business card, in the notes section of the person's contact card in your phone, or your voice memos. These notes could be comprised of anything: the most intriguing statements from your conversation, the corny jokes they told, the color of their tie, them divulging the fact that they are preparing the surprise birthday celebration for their mother who is turning sixty-seven, or the snippets of their horror story of starting as an intern. These points will come in handy later.

Another classic, yet highly memorable practice many people don't take part in anymore is the art of a handwritten note. A few days following the mixer, for example, send a thank you note recapping your conversation. Reference those fun facts you jotted down on the back of that business card and include a few when drafting a message thanking them for extending their time to you. In most instances, a business address will be present on the business card, and if not, email is fine. However, if you have chicken scratch for penmanship (you know if you do), then stick to typing up a note with a handwritten signature. Your note can go something like this:

> Dr. J,
>
> *It was such a pleasure meeting you on Sunday, March 24, 2019, at the ABCD Educational Society networking mixer. I found our conversation quite insightful. I appreciate you taking the time to provide me with tips to navigate the job application for Google as I transition out of my current industry of toy production. Also, I hope the planning is going well for your mother's 67th surprise birthday party. I look forward to staying in touch.*
>
> *Best,*
> *Saint Nicholas*

Those conversational fun facts are also important because they are transferrable to your ever-developing networking spreadsheet. This is a running log to house your professional contacts. I use Google Sheets because I can access it from anywhere with just a single login. I don't have to worry about losing contacts if my computer crashes. I prefer spreadsheet formats because they organize content in a fashion that makes it easily searchable, but any method that makes sense to you is all that matters. My spreadsheet has columns of the following fields: last name, first name, company they work for, their job title, industry, phone number, email, social media handles (if I know them), website (if applicable), how/where we met, and notes. Pretty thorough, I know, but I found it necessary for my own organizational purposes. You may modify your spreadsheet fields to have more or less of this material, but the notes section is a must-have! That is where you can place those memorable details of your conversation so that they might be helpful memory joggers when speaking with a particular person again later in your career.

The beauty of networking is that it's not only a hub for self-serving purposes. You may be the connective link for someone else's next big break. Since networking is an interconnected web, a spreadsheet acts as a phenomenal starting point to house your connections for quick reference to support someone else along their career. While making an introduction between parties may be a simple gesture of kindness, it can also make all the difference in the professional world and the opportunities afforded to those who may not have had a chance otherwise.

Going out to professional mixers and attending leadership conferences affords you the opportunity to meet other ambitious souls and build self-confidence that you are amongst that special group of people destined for greatness as well. These events provide space to showcase who you are, interact with professionals who are in your dream field, and even use them to pull the strings to get you the job at that company you've been applying to for years.

As much as I wanted to believe prospective employers were going to look at my resume and hire me contingent upon my merit, academic background, awards, and exceptional grade point average, I knew that was simply not the case. I had to get savvy talking myself into opportunities that I may not have been afforded or would be sent rejection letters otherwise. Networking and leadership conferences are the optimal opportunity to practice *selling your best self* with those elevator pitches and business cards, while positioning yourself to build a spreadsheet to be referenced for the entire duration of your working career.

After you've made initial contacts by way of networking, do your part to maintain those relationships. This isn't to say you must keep in touch every week because that's not practical. Stay in touch enough to not be forgotten. As you continue to progress in your career, you will see how quickly your networking spreadsheet will grow. These contacts aren't there to collect dust. Your connections may be the very force to change your situation. Keep your contacts informed about your latest projects and professional endeavors. Just mere conversation about your work status could spark additional connections and opportunities that would have otherwise remained unknown. Networking isn't about making an initial relationship and only calling them when needed. Networking is about actively tending to these relationships with simple calls, emails of consideration, or going out for coffee to maintain this professional web of interconnectivity. By intricately nurturing some of these relationships, you may even get a mentor out of it.

Mentors

Finding mentors is a necessary layer of the networking process. Your mentors manifest themselves in your life through internships, leadership conferences, college, networking seminars, and the like. The need for mentors never has an expiration date. Whether you are seeking support in undergrad or taking on a new position after 20 years in the workforce, as you're gaining valuable experience throughout your journey, embrace the wisdom of people who have lived what you are trying to achieve. Mentors are an educational goldmine! They have contacts, experience consistent with your field of study, and the necessary perspective to better coach you through your woes of the industry.

Mentors were a precious resource to quiet the noise around me. I had to get in touch with *credible* sources to keep me on track in a world where everyone freely comments on what they think you should do with your career, despite having no understanding of how your industry works. I had to steer clear of people who had all the answers yet, rarely had anything tangible to show for their own personal and professional efforts. It became clear to me that if I did not actively surround myself with mentors and a professional support system, then there would always be a greater amount of people in close proximity to me that would poison my well for success. It can be difficult to distance yourself from people like that, since there is naturally more of them around, especially if they are your family, peers, and sometimes, teachers. I had to remind myself that it was solely my responsibility to surround myself with people who could be a genuine resource to best offset the negativity around me. That's where my mentors came in. I allowed their industry-related feedback to ground me. If you have a good mentor, they want to meet you at the center of your thought process to better coach you through decisions that are ultimately yours to make. You may find that your mentor winds up being someone on that developing spreadsheet. However, these opportunities of connection won't manifest if you don't put yourself out there. Remember, "networking" is the one letter difference between "not working."

Chapter 8

Job Search Jumpstart

When college is all said and done, your objective is to ultimately land a job within your field of study rather quickly. While many college students reserve the job hunt until after graduation, I strongly advise against it. While I was enrolled, I consistently asked my college counterparts on the brink of graduating if they had started to apply for jobs. More than half of them were going to wait until they graduated. They never had any real explanation other than to strictly focus on school at the time. While I understood their position to a degree, I knew that was not the formula I wanted to adhere to for myself. After seeing many of them graduate and harp on the notion that they couldn't find a job, I was determined to not share in the same reality. I started applying for jobs a year and a half before completing undergrad. As backward as this may seem to some, there was always a method to my madness. I used this time as an opportunity to test out my constantly evolving resume. By circulating my resume far in advance, it not only put me on the radar of potential employers, but also opened the door to *indirectly* and *directly* gain insight about how I was presenting myself to the workforce.

When applying for jobs while still enrolled, I used that year and half to gauge if my resume was even getting traction within the applicant pool. At that point, I already developed a few versions of my resume to better identify which format worked for certain positions over others. This is important to note, as the times of employment have drastically changed. The days of one resume fitting all job postings were long over far before I even started college.

Since I was still juggling a full course load during my job search jumpstart, I kept my weekly job submissions to a minimum. Even with a small investment of my time over a year and a half, I surprisingly felt a sense of relief by being proactive with my job search. By doing so, I released myself from the all-too-common pressure of having to apply for "X" amount of jobs to land something quickly. My goal was to ensure I was the most professional version of myself on and off paper to make my job search easier upon graduation. Applying for jobs while still enrolled was the best time to obtain the necessary insight about my professional documents since I was the least defensive and unphased by the rejection emails. The intention wasn't to get a job while I was still in school. This was a chance to gain intelligence about what I could do to be more competitive in the workforce. Based on employer feedback or lack thereof, I knew if my resume was spot on or if I needed to go back to the career center and seek revisions. If I got an interview, I viewed it as a good opportunity to not only validate the strength of my resume to even qualify for a face-to-face interview, but also to test out my interview skills for positions I would truly be interested in after graduating.

While I was applying for jobs, I even took my experience a step further and connected with a few employers who rejected me. Why? I wasn't seriously looking for employment anyway. However, I wanted to understand the *why* behind their rejection. I pushed employers for greater comment beyond the dreaded generic rejection email stating, "We've decided to proceed with other applicants." I needed to know their first impressions about me as an applicant on paper. This is the feedback I needed to better equip myself and my portfolio *before* this job search got real.

Corporate rejection also exposed me to the unavoidable reality of job hunting. While many of my college counterparts couldn't understand my philosophy, I consistently stood behind what I believed to be the obvious. Wouldn't I want to find this information out about my resume *before* I graduated? Wouldn't I want to know if my resume was withstanding the workforce competition in its current state? If it wasn't, wouldn't I want to utilize the college resources afforded to me to correct these issues? These were constant questions I asked myself, all the while many of my college associates sat around asking themselves, "Why can't I get a job within my field?" Many college students fail to realize that the resources, like the career center, are factored into tuition and expire once enrollment at the college ends. It'd be a waste not to take advantage of these opportunities long before graduating since they were specifically in place to help with your job placement.

Although my communication background equipped me to become a stronger communicator and interviewer, many students may not have these same skills. College is the prime time to professionally develop yourself, practice in real interviews despite your inability to take the job (which you won't tell the employer), and affords firsthand insight on how to tackle interviews for opportunities you really want when the right time comes. If you got the job during your "trial interview" and declined it, so be it. However, if you felt insecure about how you answered some of the interview questions or disappointed with your overall delivery, honor the experience as a trial run. Talk about the pros and cons of the interview with your campus career center support or mentor, and even schedule a mock interview. This is a great way to polish your professional skills before reaching the academic finish line. Again, these are services embedded in high ass tuition fees!

I understood the foundation I was laying outside the classroom was just as critical to landing the job. By obtaining feedback from some of those employers, many organizations advised me to reach out closer to graduation to see if there was a position available. Keeping in mind that some corporate people use those remarks as passive workforce jargon to weasel out of a conversation, I also noted that such verbiage gave me leverage to confidently reach out again in the future when I was seriously looking for work. Although many employers didn't communicate with me to discuss my rejected application, to my surprise, a few others were mindful enough to share the specifics of why I either wasn't selected for an interview or not selected for the position. If the occasion presented itself for me to further discuss the rejection from the hiring manager, I found that many of them were impressed by my diligence—not settling for a generic rejection email. My goal was to demonstrate a level of professionalism, interest in the position, and develop a much-needed workforce skill, which was to embrace constructive criticism.

Naturally, my greatest critique, if you can even call it that, was my enrollment status, since I was in no position to take on a full-time job. I already expected this. Plus, I understood back then that positions are ever-changing. Job postings are dissolved, requirements and expectations are modified, or the position start date may change altogether.

Consider this. Even by applying well in advance, many employers keep an application on file for "X" amount of time. While you're in no rush to get that job because you haven't quite finished the degree needed to even qualify for the position, you never know what could manifest by simply letting the world know you are available for an opportunity. The initiative you took to set yourself apart from other applicants after being rejected, may be the very interaction that keeps your name lingering in the minds of hiring managers. After making that personal connection, tailoring your resume and interviewing skills, and giving the employer further insight on your professional goals, you may be the perfect fit for a job that arises with the organization later, and closer to your graduation date. At that point, you've positioned yourself to have an advantage over other applicants with their newly posted position because you've already established a rapport. This is the not-so-secret ingredient for a successful job search.

When developing these connections, keep in mind that they don't automatically equate to being a shoo-in for a job opportunity. Although some of the contacts I made didn't necessarily produce anything concrete, I still felt a weight lifted off my shoulders when it came to job searching. In my case, I knew myself well enough to understand that the mere thought of being unemployed stressed me out. By making myself aware of my fears, I knew if I started my job search *after* graduating, I would increase my stress-levels tremendously. Had I waited until after graduation to start applying for jobs, which is the norm for many college students, essentially, I would have started my search at ground zero when I didn't have to. I had peace in knowing that I was planting seeds to continue to put my name in the world, while also holding on to the fact that I had already planted employable seeds long before I walked across the stage. It was just a matter of time for my trees to bear fruit.

The final reason why applying for jobs early on and maximizing your campus benefits are critical to your success, boils down to good time management skills. When you are truly grinding by taking classes, working, interning, tending to personal life, and everything else in between, your college experience will be over with a blink of an eye. While managing all of that and dealing with life's unsuspecting curveballs, the last thing you want to do is not plan for the inevitable—graduation. As I consistently revisited the question of defining what drove me, one of my motivators was coming to terms with the benefits of being proactive. Schedules flip upside down, people flake on you, you're without a babysitter, you need to cover a shift, and in my case, deal with grief, as I had two deaths in my family within ten days of each other—all while academic deadlines remained constant. As college students, especially nontraditional students returning to school, you know firsthand that shit always hits the fan when you've got the most on your plate. Life has a way of crashing down when you have to study or take an exam. Chances are that term paper you've been pushing off is due or that final exam you didn't study for falls on the same day life gets in the way. By pushing myself to work on assignments, even just a little bit each day, I felt more accomplished in the work I did up to that point, which lent breathing room for me to comfortably address life's obstacles as they occurred. That is how I found balance. No one is ever exempt from life's unfortunate events, even college students. However, it's still your responsibility to best tackle every issue, without making an excuse for it. That is what college is all about, and the perfect opportunity to begin planting those seeds that start to bud into something beautiful when you complete your degree.

While taking aggressive and proactive academic and professional measures may not be everyone's cup of tea, I swear by the benefits. Looking back, I was glad I was proactive in all of my approaches. To my surprise, my degree completion date crept up on me a hell of a lot sooner than originally anticipated. Since I was double majoring, for the most part, I had quarterly meetings with my academic advisor to petition for certain classes to double count for both majors. For those who aren't aware of the general structure of an advisement appointment, this time is typically reserved for students to sit down with their academic advisor and map out the courses needed to fulfill their degree. These meetings also help determine which semester students will enroll in each course. This is a critical component to ensure you stay on course to graduate.

Trust me when I say that consistently scheduling a check-in appointment with your advisor is a timesaver and lifesaver! Between course offerings varying by the semester, degree requirement catalog changes, and every other academic variable to think of, I wanted to make sure there were as few surprises as possible when it came to completing my degree. Your advisor is there to fill in the gaps to help you reach your academic goals if they are doing their job correctly. On the other hand, students must keep this communication fluid with consistent check-ins to measure progress. A common mistake some college students make is believing they can easily modify their academic plan without the help of an advisor. Advisors are paid to plan for these changes and ensure academic success for the entire student body. Even if you feel you have your academic plan all figured out, it never hurts to get the extra verification from your advisor to be on the safe side. Under the same token though, advisors have been known to make mistakes…big ones. Unfortunately, even if your advisor is completely at fault for misguiding you, such as advising you to take an unnecessary course, or forgetting that you needed to take an additional class because your program requires it, none of that exempts a student from fulfilling the major requirements. While such errors are reprehensible, academic advisors are human, and they are juggling hundreds of personalized student academic plans. Naturally, some things fall through the cracks.

Visiting your advisor regularly ensures you're not wasting time and gives them a constant update to better assess your standing as it relates to degree completion. These appointments present advisors with multiple opportunities to catch their possible errors before students leave college, under the false assumption that they obtained their degree when they didn't. Although advisors are academic support systems, don't blindly trust your academic advisor from one meeting alone. Don't set up an advisement appointment as a freshman and not check in with them until your junior year. No one has time to take classes they don't need and pull out more aid money to cover additional classes, just to be met with, "Oops. It appears I've made an error," from an advisor!

Two of my friends pursued different degrees and left college under the impression they fulfilled all of their requirements. They were merely waiting to get their degree in the mail. One of my friends even moved across the country for a short-term opportunity that was offered to her contingent upon her being a graduate! Both friends were good about seeing their advisor, but after months of waiting for a degree to show up in the mail, they called the school and found out they were still short a class. Each of them had to return to campus and complete the requirement. Sadly, this happens way more than it should, but further validates the seriousness to have fluid communication with your advisor throughout your entire academic career.

It was spring 2017 when I scheduled another advisement appointment, under the impression I had a year left of school. I went to the appointment with all of my accumulated advisement paperwork thus far, ready to finalize my academic plan for the home stretch. My advisor started clicking on her computer for a few minutes, as I sat there in silence completely oblivious to what I was about to find out. She raised her hands from the keyboard and looked at me. She said, "It appears there's one class you took I didn't petition to be double-counted. I know you don't take classes in the summer, but by the looks of it, you'll be done with both of your major requirements in the fall." My-fucking-jaw-dropped. Caught off guard by her statement, I responded, "You mean December 2017, I'll be done with school?" She smiled and said, "Yes."

Fortunately, my advisor's error allowed me to finish school sooner rather than later, but most students aren't as fortunate. That only left me with one more semester of college when she dropped this bomb on me. While some students would kill to hear those words come out of their advisor's mouth just from pure academic burnout, I left that appointment scared shitless! Although thrilled to see the finish line a few meters away, I was still operating as if I had a year left to prepare for such a life change. Even with all the internships and submitted job applications thus far, I still didn't feel like I was ready to graduate.

After leaving that appointment I was in such shock. I called my mom and told her that I would be done with school in December. She briefly got quiet, then shouted, "Damn, already?!" Later that day I came across one of my graduate assistant instructors, Nathan. I expressed my nervousness to be done with school far sooner than I anticipated. I still felt like I wasn't enough or even good enough to take on the world. Nathan looked at me and said in his usual cut and dry manner, "That's good. I'm glad you're nervous. That means you'll do what you have to do to get a job." While Nathan and I had a history of having heated exchanges, we had a mutual respect, knowing that we were strong and resilient in our own right. He said those words so bluntly because he knew that despite my fears, I *could* and *would* withstand the pressures and curveballs that life threw my way.

Later that evening, I played back over and over again what I would have done had I still needed to find mentors, gain viable internship experience, and apply for jobs, all while still maintaining strong grades. There's no way in hell I could have effectively achieved all that in a few months' time had I started moving on those professional endeavors following this appointment. Continuing to define what drove me, my secret was simple. I always operated as if something unexpected and unaccounted for would happen, not necessarily bad things, but things I knew would divide my attention and pull me away from laying a solid foundation after undergrad. Surely enough, my unexpected life occurrence was the news that came out of the advisement appointment. Not evening knowing it, my efforts to land internships early, seek out mentors, and everything else in between was vital to best account for my unexpected tomorrow. In this case, it equated to the unanticipated graduation within a few short months.

Considering what your current responsibilities are, what can you do *within reason* to kickstart your job search jumpstart? Push yourself.

_____

_____

_____

_____

_____

Chapter 9

Don't Be a Hater

For do I now persuade men, or God? or do I seek to please men? For if I yet pleased men, I should not be the servant of Christ.

Galatians 1:10 (KJV)

Who would have thought I needed to write an entire chapter about this? Hatin'. Yet, this was an all too real demon I was battling when I was in college trying to find my way and let the world know I was hungry and eager for my chance. I remember when I was in middle school and my English teacher, Ms. Landry, elaborated on the concepts of love and hate. Ms. Landry opened the floor for comment, asking the question, "What is the opposite of love?" She posed a question to which the entire class *thought* had an obvious answer. Quite the contrary, though. In fact, the interaction stumped my entire class.

The class eagerly and confidently responded in unison, "Hate."

Ms. Landry scanned the room with her eyes, and softly said, "No. Think deeper." Some of my classmates even went as far as having a heated debate with her, adamant that what they have come to know in all of their thirteen and fourteen years of living is the notion of "hate" being "love's" antonym. After challenging us for a few minutes, we grew worn out. She went on to explain, "The real opposite of love is indifference." Based on the class' reaction, I assume none of us had been thoroughly exposed to such a term to even consider it as the answer. As we still looked at her perplexed trying to make sense of her "indifference" remark, she went on to beautifully elaborate on what it meant to love, hate, and be indifferent toward someone. The ultimate message Ms. Landry was trying to get us to understand was that love and hate, at their core, are synonymous with one another. She described love as this emotion that exudes so much energy from one person. To love someone or something requires a level of investment in your heart, mind, and soul. By loving someone, you allow that external source to have a significant impact on your mood and emotions. It's true. I mean, we've all heard the phrase, "Love can make us do some crazy things."

Now, let's think about what it means to hate someone. To hate someone requires a level of investment in your heart, mind, and soul. By hating someone, you allow that external source to have a significant impact on your mood and emotions. I'm sure hatred can make us do some crazy shit too, but I digress. You get the logic now? Although this was a concept introduced to me in middle school, it has been a topic I have given a lot of thought to over the years and developed a deeper meaning of. To love and hate someone or something, taps into emotions that reverberate along the same wavelengths. However, the truest opposite of love is indifference.

To be indifferent means that you have relinquished all concern for that individual or situation. To reach a place of indifference means you have made a subconscious or conscious commitment to place a greater emphasis on yourself and be wary of expelling energy that serves you no good. You may be asking how that's even possible in a world where everywhere you look acts as a constant reminder of where you're *not* at in your life. No matter how hard you try to catch your big break, the finish line continues to be moved. At times, it feels impossible to not feel hatred and resentment, not necessarily toward people, but agitation with the systems that make you feel as if you're not special. It was hard for me to remain indifferent in college when I was fighting for opportunity after opportunity in Los Angeles, just to be told that someone else is far more interesting than me. That can have a negative impact on your happiness and your ability to show support for other people. You may not even intend on being a "hater" but the toxic "dog eat dog" societal structure can leave you unintentionally showing a lack of support or enthusiasm for people and situations around you. You must be self-aware and brutally honest with how you feel toward others to ensure you're not the hater in the group, disguising it as indifference.

Allow me to define a hater from my scope. The term is overly used, misused, abused, and misconstrued. It's a word we typically resort to for pure convenience. Often it acts as a superficial tool to keep us from making an effort to see someone's point of view that isn't in direct alignment with our own. While hating is often reserved to describe external factors that "disrupt" us, the truth is, at its core, *hate* is sole dissatisfaction with one's self or situation. You'd be remiss to believe you've never felt this about your life at one point or another. You are a human being, and this comes with the territory of doing this thing called *life*. This in turn, means you've been a hater. If you aren't one now, you were one before.

When evaluating how my "hatred" was manifesting, it wasn't because I wasn't happy for others. It revealed itself through my own defeat, discouragement, and depression, as I was constantly under the impression I wasn't good enough. Our muddled feelings don't have anything to do with someone else's success. It's our subconscious succumbing to the pressures of life that are always telling us we should have *arrived* by now. This is especially true in the digital age of social media. It's difficult to look to the left and right of you and not compare yourself or your situation to the next person. This robs you of peace, joy, and knocks you off course from fulfilling God's ultimate plan for your life. Hence, my scripture selection for the start of this chapter. I had to understand that obtaining people's approval was never my goal. God would never use me effectively until I understood that. Let's use a different version of the verse at the start of the chapter to better understand it. Here's the New Living Translation.

> **Verse:** "Obviously, I'm not trying to win the approval of people, but of God. If pleasing people were my goal, I would not be Christ's servant" (Galatians 1:10)

When I reflected on my life and constantly played back in my head what I envisioned for myself after college, I couldn't act like it was all a cakewalk and a motivational experience. I often found myself angry, bitter, resentful, and constantly questioning why I was continuing to push forward in the media industry. Many of the opportunities I wanted were lined with the names of those who already had an existing public image; were reserved for people with famous parents and were positioned in the limelight from birth; or, were for those who were willing to seal the deal with a kiss and sleep their way to the top. No matter what the reason, I found myself pissed off more often than not! From the outside, I appeared to have had it all together and a promising future, but the reality was, I too, harbored loads of hatred and animosity in my heart. It grew significantly, especially by way of the growing digital era, as I witnessed others with a fraction of my potential simply have major opportunities fall in their lap because they sold their soul for a couple hundred thousand followers.

I didn't hate or envy anyone in particular. I really despised *the system* that put certain individuals in positions to be favored with not enough reason to show for it. But hell, that's a life lesson within itself, given that this is the norm in just about any industry you decide to go into. However, it didn't change the fact that it deeply bothered me.

If you are the "It" girl at the time, you're hired. No one was checking for me. Like you, I'm only human, and I naturally grew frustrated thinking about this given that while in undergrad, I had easy access to some of these celebrities or *pseudo-celebs* when I interned in Los Angeles. Despite not always showing on the exterior, I consistently felt discouraged knowing that even though I loved school and had no intentions of dropping out, my passion, talent, and education were simply not enough to even be considered for the opportunities I so desperately wanted in the entertainment and broadcast industry. I vividly remember feeling the sensation as if I swallowed a giant hippo pill with no water, gasping for air as dryness coated my throat when I saw people on television hosting gigs because of their family name, offered the job because of who they were adjacent to in Hollywood, or because they gained a massive following on social media. Here I was, working my ass off in school, being trained to interview, shoot, edit, and produce my content, yet I was left feeling inadequate, nonetheless. I've seen some celebs, many of whom I've met (some nice and others rude), with no formal coaching, education, or training, go on TV and read off teleprompters like robotic and illiterate bimbos. But the networks and organizations *must* have them at that red carpet to ride that public relations wave of whatever or whoever is gaining the most media attention at the time. Although not right, it only made sense that I would be upset. What's a girl to do?! It's no secret that it's difficult to stand out in this industry, especially in LA. It's even harder to stand out as a black woman willing to hold firm to her morals and values without being seen as "difficult" or "aggressive," but that's a topic for another book. I couldn't help but constantly question what I was working toward, knowing that many of the job opportunities didn't have Alexis Thrower's name on it. So, I write this chapter, from a place of not merely preaching to you, but recognizing and acknowledging my hatred that I once had for this industry, in general.

Where do I go from here? What am I supposed to do with these thoughts and feelings? These were golden questions that played a role in evaluating my life—helping me better figure shit out!

Beyond life simply not being fair, it finally hit me. I don't even remember what I was doing, but I recall having an epiphany that stopped me completely in my tracks. I finally realized the root of my bitterness. I was growing more insecure with the rapidly changing digital era that placed (and still places) more value and affords greater opportunities for people willing to divulge *every* aspect of their life for a few minutes of fame. Our world primarily values everything that isn't real. The general culture of this industry maintains the same emphasis it always has. It's just worse now that cameras and phones are an integral part of our day to day. Now, I'd be lying if I told you I didn't get m fair share of chuckles from social media. I can also see some of the professional benefits it presents. However, it also acts as a hub to showcase manufactured lives that give people an unhealthy amount of attention. We waste so much time envying people who only give the *appearance* that their life is all gravy, when it's not. While those social media celebs spend hours to capture the *perfect* image for their followers to obsess over, we look at these pictures, baffled at what we're doing wrong because our lives aren't panning out the same way. The truth is, in many cases, their life isn't fulfilling to them either.

I was seeing the correlation of these rising social media celebs doing a whole lot of nothing but cashing in on all the opportunities that I was pursuing a four-year degree for. They were interviewing celebs on the red carpet, getting mentorships from major industry professionals, hosting gigs, landing digital content talent opportunities, and then some. These were all the things I was seeking but wasn't sacrificing my morals to get there. This is where my bitterness started to kick in, as it seemed like a requirement to compromise my values in order to make any real traction in this industry. I didn't know if I was capable of giving up some of the more precious things in life, like my privacy and genuine intimacy with others to achieve these dreams. More questions started to consume my thoughts. *Was this life really for me? Was I operating in my purpose? Could I be happy with myself when the cameras were off? Could I live in a life where I was not seeking validation from social media notifications telling me one more person liked my image? Could the industry even be receptive to this regular girl without the high maintenance façade that is often associated with women working in the business? Would people see me for me or see what they want to see? Could I make it by being authentically me without anyone trying to change me?* Yes, I have my "boujee" girl moments that command more attention at times, but for the most part, I am, and have always been a Plain Jane. That kind of girl isn't typically on the radar of people who "matter."

I'm the girl who likes to go to a concert and watch the performance on the stage, and not through my camera lens. Half of my social media is flooded with pictures of my little niece and nephews and me looking a hot ass mess, because that's the honest representation of my reality when I'm with my family. I'm the girl who just needs a spoon with a single scoop of vanilla or strawberry ice cream. I don't like all those extra toppings and shit on my dessert. The simple chicks aren't the ones who society says gets the job, especially in the news and media industry. Plain Janes don't stand out. They get cast as extras, backups, understudies, or overlooked altogether, in almost every aspect of their life. But don't feel bad for me. Even when I didn't have all the answers to these questions as I was figuring things out, my gut was saying I was taking the right steps that God wanted me to. So, while doing my best to hold on to those Plain Jane morals, I naturally started to make peace with trusting God's plan for me even when society was telling me otherwise. Knowing that and pushing myself to better define the pillars of my integrity, I wanted everything I did and whatever I touched to be significant. I wanted someone to hire me solely because I was trained and qualified to do the job. Even before graduating, I knew I wanted employers to extend an offer because they saw potential and recognized the foundation I laid to only get better in my craft. I never wanted someone to measure my success by the viewership I could bring to their network simply because I acted a damn fool online or was half-naked in the majority of my social media posts. I'm not knocking anyone else who has done it, but I wanted and expected far more for myself. Whatever I did, I wanted it to be… timeless.

Before we continue, let's take a moment to think about what or who you're hating on. I understand that's a bold statement, but no one has to see this but you. This question requires you to be brutally honest with yourself. No one likes to think of themselves as a hater, and it's even harder to murmur the truth about our not-so-pleasant ways of thinking, but it's got to be done. When doing this exercise, I want you to do so without heavily considering the negative connotation to the word "hate." Just write and be honest about what makes you tick. Just like my case, it wasn't a person or type of person I hated. I hated the politics of the system that "put people on." For you to get past the hump of what's holding you back from unlocking your full potential, it requires you to be honest with the external factors surrounding your life that keep you concerned about everything and everyone else. *What* or *who* is it that keeps you defeated, causing you to forget how awesome you are? You can write full sentences or bullet points. Once you take some time for deep reflection, we can move on to the next phase of how to handle those feelings.

_____

_____

_____

_____

_____

After having some tough conversations with myself (as I hope you also did with yourself above), and pinpointing the underlying reason for my discontent with the industry structure, I had to be proactive in finding solutions to address my issues. I had to decipher what I could and could not change to give myself clarity about what to pray on to better determine my next steps. If I didn't do so, it was just a matter of time before the negativity I felt internally was going to reveal itself on the surface. I remember at times being salty as hell, working as hard as I did, being treated like scum at an internship, working multiple jobs to put myself through school, juggling family life, and giving one hundred percent in every aspect of my life just to still come up short. This was a toxic headspace to be in and would ultimately hinder my ability to confidently walk in the plans that God had for me. I needed to find that level of indifference that I discussed earlier.

I forced myself into God's presence, receiving the gentle reminder that what's mine is mine, including all of my career opportunities. I had to grow indifferent to what everyone else was doing because He promised I would be destined for great things all along, especially if I was doing my part to consistently develop myself in any of my respective roles.

So what was my treatment plan following my self-diagnosis of pure negativity? In short, the prescription was to fill my plate. It didn't matter if I already had a jam-packed schedule juggling full-time units, extracurricular activities, and everything else in between. Truth be told, if I had time to be that consumed with what everyone else had going for them, that meant I had far too much time on my hands. Knowing that tidbit of information about my life, was enough for me to reexamine my own goals and objectives. It was just me, my pen, and my paper, redefining the expectations I was holding myself to while in college and after undergrad. I created schedules and wrote down on pieces of paper what I wanted to achieve. I swore by my planner! I would create daily, weekly, and monthly checklists and consistently revise them accordingly. Planners may not work for everyone, but I found that by keeping them filled, and always having some sort of plan, even if things didn't always pan out the way I wanted them to, I was growing more fixated on achieving whatever the next task was on *my* agenda. Couple that with writing down my newfound life expectations in a journal and on sticky notes everywhere, the next thing I knew, I organically stopped having time to concern myself with anything or anyone else. When I journaled, I never used it as a time to view anyone as a competitor. It was simply a way to combat negativity by flushing out my thoughts and fears. I also used it as an outlet to practice self-love. Writing down the expectations I was setting for my life was a way to create the space to remind myself of what I was capable of, especially with God on my side. By transferring everything I envisioned I could do with myself and my time on paper, I pushed myself to even greater limits and didn't listen when people told me to slow down. Looking back, some of my life goals and objectives were completely out of reach at the time, and I probably could have taken a few more pauses to catch my breath, but that's okay because they were my goals, and I was hungry to achieve them by any means necessary.

While I learned that I may have been too hard on myself at times, I also believed that like a diamond, there was still a beauty in the pressure-filled development stages of such a prized jewel. By trying to reach such exceedingly difficult goals, I lacked the time and energy required to focus on my inadequacies by way of comparing myself to anyone. I wasn't even giving anyone or anything a second thought because I was fixated on getting my shit together.

Comparison is a natural human response, which to some degree, I believe aids in how we make sense of the world. While comparison is necessary to provide a general outline of what you should and shouldn't do, it should never be done at the expense of degrading yourself and your worth. That's when that negative self-talk starts to kick in. When I made a hard shift with setting my own exceedingly high and difficult goals without comparison to anyone else, that's when I found my aura of indifference. Anything that happened around me that wasn't consistent with me reaping benefits, especially in my field of study, I stopped giving it so much attention. I stopped caring about the Instagram models and comedians who weren't directly responsible for the opportunities that were meant or not meant for me. I stopped worrying about the celebrity who got that gig I went after. I ignored the slick, hatin' ass remarks family and acquaintances had to say about the way I decided to live my life, simply off the strength of me wanting more and better for myself. I became a pro at tuning out people who used phrases like, "She thinks she better than everybody else," "Oh, you know she's boujee," or my personal favorite, "She thinks since she got that little degree she know everything." While it was evident that the root of their hatred was disappointment in themselves for not having the courage to figure their own shit out, I still had to find a way to purge myself of that toxic energy so I would not exude that to others. If I wasn't careful, poor energy would rub off on me, make me a hater, and block my future blessings. In fact, those remarks were the very thing that kept me determined to keep my planner filled so I always had a viable reason to not be around the very negativity that could transfer and cause me to exhibit that same hate for others and their success.

When I was reestablishing who I wanted to be and coming to understand who God called me to be, most of my life was comprised of remaining focused on those God-ordained goals. I can see looking back now that He was putting me through obstacles to develop my skills to be a servant for Him. The challenges I was tasked with were separate than anyone else's, as I was being built for longevity, not temporary recognition. The picture was becoming clearer about what my next steps needed to be in my journey. My path was going to be eventful, jam-packed. It left me with no time to concern myself with others, despite yearning for some of the same opportunities that I saw the pseudo-celebs obtain. I became so swamped with the physical and spiritual assignments on my plate, that I didn't have an ounce of time left to hate on, speak ill of, or watch what anyone else was doing. I just kept doing what I felt I was supposed to do without appeasing anyone. That's why the opening Bible verse of this chapter spoke to my heart when thinking about the responsibility we owe to ourselves. Regardless of your faith, our job is to be concerned with the tasks we've been assigned.

Going out your way to please people who aren't even easy to please, is not your calling. People won't understand why you're distant at times, as they quickly write you off as a hater because you're not fawning over that celebrity on the red carpet. They won't understand your work ethic, your growth, or why you work so hard in and out of the classroom. They can't comprehend that distance makes for increased silence for you to gain clarity about what your next move will be, all the while they sit on the sidelines and talk shit about what you're doing. These reverberating voices of negativity, also known as your haters, won't phase you. The places you are going are positive manifestations of you exposing yourself to experiences that allow you to see what you were led to do. Once you've found your rhythm, setting your goals and objectives for your life becomes apparent, and it won't matter what a hater has to say. Those same people will be completely oblivious that you are on assignment to do something "superstar-worthy" in your own right, even if you are still trying to determine what it is.

When I was writing out my list of life goals and objectives, the two most important ones came to mind. The most obvious one being that I followed the steps of this book to land a job within my field of study. The second was becoming unapologetic in cutting people off. When I heard those bullshit ass remarks about me being "better than everyone else" or "uptight" because I wasn't conducting myself in a manner that mirrored their behavior, I realized I didn't have to continue to subject myself to unnecessary ridicule. I was coming to terms with the fact that I couldn't please everyone, which further thrusted me into the space of indifference. Be prepared, though. I would be doing you a disservice if I did not acknowledge that your journey may make for a lonely one as well. While establishing my worth and locking in on the plans God had for me, I couldn't take everyone with me. Although my presentation of how I handled life may have been *polished* to most, it was not all glitz and glamour. There *were* and will forever be extra-long days that lead into many silent and tearful nights. Tears of joy and pain, leaving you walking through a dark jungle that not even those closest to you could ever understand. God forbid I tried to articulate what I was going through, just to be written off as being "too young to be so stressed" and "dramatic" for trying to talk out my jumbled thoughts because I'm "far more fortunate than most to be able to go to college," as if no issues arise while attending. Although I stopped entertaining those remarks, the feedback from my haters taught me a very valuable lesson. While at times I was down, yearning for the people closest to me to be by my side, that isolation revealed peace. It showed me that chaos found its way to me based on the people I allowed to get comfortable enough in my space. I learned to fall in love with the quiet. To my surprise, the distance that came with cutting people off who weren't in alignment with my life, was the very thing that showed me how valuable my peace was and that it was solely my responsibility to protect it.

I started to conceal and even protect the most painful parts of my experiences because small-minded people, including so-called friends and family members, would never understand the bigger obstacles God was preparing me for. Sometimes all I needed was a hug, not cold-hearted, dismissive, and downright belittling comments. If I had to pick the single most difficult part of my journey, that would be it. I wanted my entire family to be on board with me. I wanted them to support my growth just as much as I pushed for theirs. As I continued to mature mentally, spiritually, and emotionally, it started to make sense, though. A biological connection or a lifelong *friend* does not exempt them from being your haters.

Let's take a second to talk about you. Haters can come in all forms. To better identify them, you have to make yourself aware of your own flaws. For the first part of this exercise, jot down what you do or things you may say that can have some hater undertones. Like my case, it doesn't have to be a particular person. It can be general societal elements, like social media. What factors make you feel insecure about what you're doing with your life? Be honest with yourself. The second part of this exercise is to identify your haters. Whether that be family, friends, or co-workers, consider the people who have far more negative remarks to say about your life than positive. Don't forget to jot down the people who make those sly passive aggressive comments as well. Lastly, after you've examined yourself and those around you, what newfound goals and objectives do you intend on setting for yourself to ensure these factors don't hinder your performance?

_____

_____

_____

_____

_____

When I created this bubble of only concerning myself with my operations, I became much more supportive of others. I was already a cheerleader for my friends, but after some further reflection, I felt an even greater increase of support for those close to me, as well as strangers. This was attainable because I finally grasped that what truly belonged to me, was only mine. Exuding hate helped no one. It didn't make me feel better. It didn't afford me better opportunities. It didn't put extra money in my pocket. If anything, it just robbed me of the peace I was trying so desperately to protect.

My visual excitement to see others win without concern for what "leg up" they had, changed the climate for what *could* and *would* attract to me. I naturally found God putting people directly in my path, who were meant to be there to take me to the next level. Some people were there to challenge me, while others were only there for a season. Some people fell in my path to connect me with others who could help further my career. It all came with me having the right attitude and mentality to embrace it all because I left no empty space to hate on anyone else or envy their blessings.

Chapter 10

Fast Before You Ask

Although we've had some fun with this read (and took a few jabs at people's pride), as you have seen throughout this book, I humbly acknowledge I am nothing without my faith. While you're navigating the waters of early adulthood and college life, your foundation for landing a job within your field goes beyond your actions in the physical realm. Having a spiritual foundation helps better balance the chaos of our lives and reinforces what our calling is in a world full of uncertainties. Even for those who aren't religious, there's no denying the need to attain some sense of direction in a world that forces us to second guess our purpose. This is especially true when social media acts as a constant hub to spotlight false representations of reality. We've grown accustomed to living a life where people only post their wins, misleading us to wrongfully correlate that those individuals have it "all figured out." How can we possibly focus on what we've got going on when everyone else is working overtime to make us *think* they have it going on? This creates an even greater sense of depression and confusion when trying to seek out confirmation of our calling.

This is a dangerous world to find ourselves in; becoming prisoners of our minds questioning whether our value and contributions to this world are not only "right" but wondering whether it's even enough. Now, imagine all of these thoughts palpitating at the forefront of your psyche while you're taking your last set of final exams. That was me. There I was pairing these anxiety-stricken emotions with being a first-generation college student, living an experience none of my family members truly understood. I was a bundle of nerves and needed a moment to simply surrender—surrender my thoughts, anxiety, family responsibilities, and surrender everyone's expectations of me. I needed a moment to *not* be someone's role model. I needed a few moments to not be a failure in the eyes of myself.

For me, finishing undergrad was about getting myself together when no one was watching. I was preparing in every aspect of the word—mentally, physically, emotionally, and spiritually. A new chapter of my life was about to begin, and although I hadn't solidified any employment plans just yet, I embraced the change to come in just a matter of weeks. I knew I needed to do something different before my undergraduate career came to an end. I just didn't know what. Then, at the beginning of finals week, I felt a fluttering sensation coat the pit of my stomach. God's voice gently whispered, "Fast before you ask." Before I could even utter any further words, I said, "Thank you, Lord," because only He knew just how many requests I was about to ask Him for after graduating. "Fast before you ask for anything, Alexis."

For those who don't know what fasting is, it is a spiritual and religious practice of abstaining from certain goods. It's primarily to abstain from food but fasting can be done for virtually anything—food, soda, TV, social media, and the list goes on. Some people fast for health reasons, such as drinking only water because your doctor ordered lab tests, or simply fasting for detox purposes. In my particular case, on my last day of undergrad, I chose to abstain from food and only drink water until I had dinner with my dad that night. I also chose to reduce my social media use during this time, recognizing the way it was making me feel when I would log on and see such *fake* activity. It jacked me up emotionally, feeling like the world was telling me I'm behind the curve in life.

As for me, I fasted as a token of trust. I fasted to surrender my anxieties to the Lord, because I believed I did what I was supposed to do and then some in college, as a result of following all of the steps in this book. Now, it was simply a matter of getting out of my own way and letting Him work.

For the first time in my four and a half years of undergrad, I felt an inner peace radiate over my body. I knew that through my diligence in school, I had laid it all down at the altar, so to speak. I comfortably relaxed in the truth that I ceased every moment, every internship, networking experience, and academic exchange both in and out of the classroom. This is my hope and prayer for all college grads. This is the plateau of peace you *should* have approaching graduation. This isn't necessarily because you have a formal job offer, or even because you have multiple employers making contact with you, as was my case. The peace stems from *expecting* reaped benefits because you sowed and tended to seeds that produced the best fruits possible. You didn't plant apple seeds expecting oranges to grow. In school, you didn't hope that by simply going through the motions of getting the degree, it was sufficient for success after graduating. Your success is deemed by planting that apple seed, and actively catering to the soil to ensure you produced great apples. Metaphorically and literally speaking, you'd make for a shitty grower if all you did was plant the seeds. Your success will be inevitable because unlike many of your college counterparts, you understand that you can't plant a seed and expect it to grow on its own merit. Not one farmer or gardener I know obtained a harvest by not watering, pruning, and ensuring the necessary sunlight was given to their crops. They faithfully gave their plant the needed love and care it required, so the crops could work for them. You ought to be doing the same thing within your college career.

My fast was a way to say, "thank you" to God for revealing these steps (seeds) to me. Like most farmers, the goods produced are often distributed to benefit mass amounts of people. I fasted to thank God that I went through all of this to give others a guidebook that I didn't have along my journey.

Fasting may be foreign to you at first, but it wouldn't hurt to try, especially when you are expecting something major to happen in your life. As a child I saw my mom fast, so the experience wasn't new for me personally, but a challenge at times, nonetheless. As I spiritually matured, I realized the more I fasted to purge my body of negative toxins, the more clarity I had. Surprisingly, I was much more in tune and receptive to the experiences happening around me. I came to understand that even though I was getting a degree for a job specifically within my field, it didn't necessarily mean I would work in that industry forever. It was a matter of me being intentional with my life and my studies, that I later came to realize I never truly had a dream job. My education, at the core, revealed that my passion revolved around using my learned communication skills to be a liaison to effectively disseminate important information to the masses, especially for students who look like me. With that, I found my skills would be welcomed in various fields, even if the focus wasn't communications-specific. By being my own greatest educational advocate, that passion acted as a foundational stepping stone to reveal my other passions and callings. So, while you read this book as you work toward your degree, even if you change fields later, understand you are able to shift directions effectively because you still acted with purpose based on the skills you were gaining at the time. All of these experiences come full circle to reveal what you are destined to do long-term. The picture of your life will become clearer as you continue to constructively build on the skills you already have. Even if you start working in your field and end up in another industry later, the degree itself wasn't a waste. It's ultimately up to you to maximize the opportunities associated with the degree you majored in and find applicability and transferability with those skills.

Now, what about those students who are finishing school who know deep down they half-assed their work through college? They are the ones who have a foggier view of what they're doing afterward. They may be the ones who hated what they majored in and didn't even fathom exploring anything else because school just didn't situate itself well in their life, regardless of the major. Unfortunately, this is common for many college students, and another reason I felt compelled to write this book. If that's you or someone you know, I advise you to examine how much time you have left in school and reevaluate what *realistic* adjustments you can make during the remainder of your college journey. Fasting can help with this, as it has a way of revealing some things to you that may be beneficial before graduating.

To couple with fasting, start connecting with people who are in alignment with you spiritually. After you've done everything possible academically, pray that God will light your path and connect you with people who will validate that all your hard work leading up to this point will not go unnoticed. Tap into this base for support, not just upon graduating, but all throughout college. My youth pastor, Teach, was someone I used as a resource when I battled life's challenges while I was enrolled. When I needed to cry, pray, talk about family chaos, or seek religious advice when navigating uncharted territory in my day-to-day operations, I called Teach. With his support, I was able to find that spiritual balance. In addition to that, I sought out a journalism mentor who also shared my beliefs. His name is Kevin John, a sports anchor. Although I only knew a handful of sports terms, I relied on his input heavily during my transitional period from college to the workforce, because he went through what I was about to sign up for. This divine meeting of the minds gave me a coach to navigate the industry while obtaining a wealth of knowledge that I would have never had without him.

Having a seasoned professional already working in my field of interest to speak with was integral to my job search. As I started applying for jobs at television stations, Kevin was already familiar with them or knew someone who worked there. In fact, his insight about certain stations helped me dodge some major bullets. His support allowed me to better hone in on the bigger picture by considering opportunities that I would have otherwise overlooked. The deal was even sweeter, because every conversation ended with Kevin saying he was going to pray for me—calming my anxiety knowing that I had someone else praying for my success, just as much as I was fighting for my own. I wouldn't have experienced the beauty in that had I not put myself out there to make those connections.

In this book, I've only scratched the surface of the few things that you could do to make the most out of your time left in college. This work can't be done overnight, but you shouldn't underestimate the power of what you can achieve in one academic year. No matter what decision you make for yourself, remember, you are not a lost cause. If you can make these adjustments in one school year, imagine the groundwork you can lay in four. Hopefully, with this book finding you when it did, you still have some time in your academic career to make things right for yourself, especially if you actively apply these steps to your life. Only you can examine your current situation and know the appropriate measures needed to change some of your circumstances. It boils down to what you are willing to do, independent of what others will say.

I strongly believe that when pursuing our career endeavors post-college, our responsibility is to be of service to others. In doing so, we learn more about ourselves, our morals, values, and real aspirations in life. I believe that in serving others from the stance of working for a corporation, volunteering, or interning, even if short-lived, is how we are led to find out what our ultimate purpose is.

As for me, I am a firm believer that true faith comes from your walk with God. True faith is how you conduct yourself with the Lord when no one is watching. True faith is believing He has an ordained purpose for your life, and it is our responsibility to seize every opportunity. By doing so, we find out exactly what He wants us to do with ourselves. True faith is not merely speaking to God when we want something. True faith, to me, means that everyone else's walk is none of our damn business! True faith is asking God to reveal the lesson He wants you to take from each situation, believing that it will become abundantly clear how you can be a vessel for something bigger than yourself. Faith to me is about serving others, only wanting in return the experience of learning more about yourself to better pinpoint your God-ordained calling.

So, how did my fasting come into play with these spiritual principles? Well, there I was during finals week, reaffirming to myself that I would fast on the last day of undergrad, all while thinking more critically about what I wanted for myself, and being very specific about it. People often take for granted how specific you need to be when asking God to work wonders in your life, especially to address the key reason why you picked up this book, which is to start your career within your field of study immediately following college. Going to God with a vague request will manifest a vague reality. Let's examine a prayer as an example.

> *Lord, I really need a job. I'm tired of this minimum wage kick and now that I have this degree, I'm ready to make a decent living. Please grant me a job somewhere ASAP.*

While I won't call this prayer bogus, it certainly doesn't give God much to work with and sure as hell doesn't help you get clear about the desires of your heart. Some people feel this kind of prayer is sufficient because God is the Almighty Creator who already has a plan for your life. Some people may think because God already knows the direction He wants to take you in, there's no reason to pray any harder. I have two things to say about that. For starters, contrary to popular belief, God gives us choices and free will. While He may have an ultimate destination for our lives and has the capacity to keep us in certain uncomfortable situations for whatever reason, He still presents us with the opportunity to have a choice about how some of our circumstances pan out. It's in *our* decision-making that we become better human beings, who learn from our mistakes and maximize the opportunities before us to be the people we were called to be. This is far easier said than done. We've all been there in some form or fashion—actively making the wrong decision because it *felt* right in the moment. Maybe you were falling in love with someone who you knew in your gut was no good for you—running behind them distracted from your studies, leaving you emotionally drained with your broken heart in both hands. Maybe you felt the social pressure to conform to a reckless lifestyle that goes completely against what you want for yourself but do everything in your power to sabotage your educational ticket out because the street life seems familiar to what you witnessed growing up. Throughout all of this chaos, you still had some choices. What I've learned through my own experiences is that while I pray to God that He consistently guides my path, I too, am personally responsible for protecting my destiny. This comes from the decisions I make and the company I keep.

The second point to consider when praying is that lacking specificity about our wants and needs can leave our prayers answered, but with an outcome still unsatisfactory to what we really envisioned. God could give you *exactly* what you asked for, in the *exact* form in which you asked it, but being the selfish beings we are, we often get salty behind the Holy verdict. With that same prayer, the department of waste management may call you to work as a sanitation worker. I mean you *did* say you wanted a job. You got an offer. You're tired of working minimum wage. Sanitation employees can make a decent living. The job came rather quickly like you wanted. God responded to that prayer, as it was requested. You should be happy, right? You're probably not. So, let's examine your prayer a little more. Nowhere in your prayer did you specify that the diploma you worked ever so hard for was even a requirement for the job you wanted. Let the department of waste management call you with a job after you got your *fancy* degree and you're pissed! While this isn't to pass judgment on the respectable men and women who work tirelessly to keep our streets clean and well maintained, some college graduates think that type of work is now beneath them yet, couldn't keep that same energy when asking God for what they wanted in a job in the first place. Just something to think about. Specificity helps you get clear of what you really want and makes for a powerful combination when you fast.

Amid my final exams and fasting, I found that I was better able to envision and tailor my prayer in the most articulate way possible. My prayer didn't contain exaggerated scholarly terms. If anything, it was probably one of my most simplistic prayers. I attribute that to my mind and body being figuratively and literally clearer by way of minimizing my social media use and abstaining from toxic food we eat every day. I remember talking to God as a friend. My prayer went a little something like this.

> Lord, this is it. I am a day away from finishing undergrad. I first want to say, thank you. Had it not been for you I would not have been able to overcome it all while juggling full-time course units and working all the hours I did. God, I know you did not bring me this far, simply to bring me this far. Lord, you know the root of my anxiety. You know I desire to accomplish so much. Lord, I have done my due diligence in school, and although I am not sure which opportunity you have called me to do, please guide me. I know I majored in the right field and I trust that with my resume being out in the world as extensively as it is, you will guide me to the right communication and/or journalistic opportunity. God, you know my strengths and weaknesses to a tee, as you created me. God, not only am I believing you, but as a small token of my faith, tomorrow (my last day of undergrad) I give my body to you through my spiritual fast. I fast for you Lord, not merely because I am walking in the expectation for good things to happen for me, but as a gesture of my appreciation for everything you have done and for bringing me this far. Lord, I thank you in advance for all that you are about to do in my life, as you will reveal more opportunities or provide me with confirmation about where you want me to go immediately. I believe this is the right timing for an abundance of opportunities to come my way, so much so that I will have to **decline** offers because I'll have my pick at whichever opportunity I want. I just need your confirmation of the place you want me to be. More importantly, Lord, I trust you.

Do you see the difference in the two prayers? While my prayer wasn't specifically focused on the logistics of where I wanted to work, how much money I wanted to make, and where I wanted to live, I knew that wasn't the time for that type of prayer. At this particular milestone in my life, graduating from college, the more appropriate prayer was one demonstrating complete trust in God's plan, which is extremely difficult for a control freak like myself. I knew if I didn't surrender, I would still be spinning my wheels doing something completely unrelated to what I went to school for, like a lot of students. I'm not saying my words are the greatest prayer, but it was perfect to Him.

Now that you understand specificity is key with what you're asking God for following graduation, take some time to write down your prayer to God or your specific expectations from the universe. I foresee you needing a little more space than the other reflection pieces, but by all means, grab an extra sheet of paper, if necessary.

_____

_____

_____

_____

_____

While my prayer for you is that all you asked for manifest itself in due time, I also don't want us to overlook the fact that prayer, fasting, motivational guidebooks, or whatever other methods you take part in to get you to the next level, are not indicators that adversity will not come your way. If anything, the more you ask for, the more adversity will find you. On the flip side of the coin, be aware. By being so detailed in your prayer, you may become overwhelmed if God gives you all you asked for at once, or disappointed if He doesn't. All of that brings me to referencing a passage from an old book gifted to me from my Auntie Gail when I graduated high school, which perfectly found me again after finishing undergrad. The book is titled *Life's Principles for the Graduate: Nine Truths for Living God's Way* by Charles F. Stanley. One of the passages is titled "Tough Training" and explores the caveats of adversity when you are walking in your purpose. It spoke about the topic so beautifully, I had to share a bit of it here.

> *Adversity is one of life's inescapable experiences... God has advanced His greatest servants through adversity, not prosperity... We may wonder, 'Lord, what on earth are You doing?'...If our lives were free from persecution or trials—if we had everything we wanted and no problems—what would we know about our heavenly Father?... Adversity can be a deadly discouragement or God's greatest tool for advancing spiritual growth. Your response can make all the difference. Remember that God has a purpose for the hardship He's allowed, and it fits with his wonderful plan for your life (p.102-103).*

You spot that word "servant" again? What about, "*Your* response can make all the difference," referencing your ability to make your own decision, even if life gets messy. What more can *you* do to make the difference in your own life?

Frustrated that I wouldn't land a tv broadcast internship *before* I graduated, one of my television and film instructors, Professor Bloom, told the class about a Cal State L.A. alum and former student of his who had recently been honored for her work at KTLA 5 News. Once I got her name, I hunted her down. Although the likelihood of landing another internship before I graduated was unlikely, it was still worth having a conversation with her. We chatted by phone and she said she would pass my information along to the corresponding people. At that point, I pressed on with my coursework for my last semester.

Before sharing the specifics of the full-time job offer I ultimately accepted, in January, following undergraduate completion, I participated in the month-long consecration with my church. Although I was already in talks and negotiating with employers at this time, I still felt as if I came up short by not having a television broadcast internship. Surely enough, while submitting my body to God during this time, on January 17, 2018, I heard a very faint voice in my head say, "You're going to hear from KTLA 5 tomorrow."

I didn't think anything of it when those words initially crossed my mind. It was so faint, I forgot about it. To my surprise, the very next day, the assistant news director for KTLA 5 called offering me a television broadcast internship! It wasn't before I graduated, but still a major win! Then, I remembered that voice that whispered to me the day before, understanding that God's approach to reaching us is sometimes ever so subtle, that we have to do our part to listen. My bodily commitment through fasting gave Him the required space to show up and show out in my life. This reinforced the words God told me months earlier, which was to "fast before I ask." Not only did God align it so that I would soon be landing a job within my field, but I also landed a news internship in Los Angeles (market #2) to give me the additional and much-needed training to better prepare myself for my journalistic and communication-based journey ahead.

Now, let's rewind to my final exam week. After being more specific with my prayer requests, committing to fasting, and temporarily limiting my social media use to think more clearly, the Thursday before my last final, God kicked in full force. God acknowledged that I had gotten out of my own way and trusted Him to work. Employers started contacting me for jobs, internships, and interviews, all consistent with a journalism and/or communication background while I was still one day shy from completing undergrad. I hadn't even started my fast for the day as I initially planned to do on the Friday of my last final!

While I was over the moon from these calls and emails, that attention, in turn, evoked a whole new level of anxiety, stemming from not wanting to make the wrong choice. Many of the employers who contacted me were from out of state, and being a true California girl, I wasn't all that impressed to relocate away from my family and the fabulous California sunshine. Some of the opportunities were even television broadcast internships out of state, but just didn't feel right or didn't pay at all! I was talking to myself, wondering how I could be so ungrateful when my phone literally kept ringing from people reaching out for possible job opportunities, all while I was still working my way through final exams! I had to remind myself that I was getting what I prayed for. I wanted an abundance of options that would force me to decline offers so that I could make the right choice. In true Alexis fashion though, I still found time to sulk, feeling like a failure because I didn't want to make the wrong decision out of the many opportunities that attracted to me. Even with that, I kept praying that God would handle it because He and I both knew I worked too hard to come up short.

If you are anything like me and are fixated on your flaws, you forget to give yourself credit for your accomplishments. Although I had tons of people in my corner who constantly reminded me how great I was doing and how accomplished I was becoming, it was still hard for me to receive words of encouragement because I was so hard on myself (and still am).

As my last day of undergrad arrived, and I began my fast, I solely latched on to the conversations between me and God. I knew all the pieces were coming together as they were supposed to. There was no other option but for things to work out in my favor since I was praying about my career and was confident that I exhausted every possibility to have the right people make contact with me, and the wrong people keep their distance.

God reminded me of something He placed on my heart a few years back. I rarely had people call or text me. My phone was so dry I used to get excited seeing a text notification, just to open it up with a message from my mom asking me to pick up a white onion from the grocery store. I used to constantly question myself and doubt my social skills since my hotline never blinged! It also didn't help that I had an annoying little sister swearing up and down the block I didn't have friends. God said, "Your phone is not supposed to be tied up, Alexis. I need your line free. When you hear it, get excited because you'll know it's an opportunity I have put in place for you." God couldn't best work under the conditions of me being caught up in social media and wasting a day on foolishness if I was sitting on my ass, not being productive in figuring out my purpose. I mean, why should He work hard to make wonders happen for us if we're not working to make more happen for ourselves? Once I understood that, doors started opening for me.

Although I primarily abstained from food, some of us may need a fast from other aspects of our life to hear God more clearly so that we might fulfill the opportunities He has in front of us. It may be food, it may be social media that you need to disconnect from for a while, or step away from a relationship that you will see in time was toxic and preventing you from reaching your full potential. Sometimes we must purge ourselves from overly consuming external sources that interfere with our blessings. Just remember, when you eliminate these things, do so without dragging your feet. Do so with the utmost amount of purpose and passion that you are finding out who you are and what your responsibilities are in this lifetime. Fasting is a course of action for *your* benefit.

When I woke up that Friday morning committed to my fast as I embarked on my last final, I said, "God, I thank you in advance for all that you have done for me and all that you will do for me. I fast today walking in the expectation for good things and I merely need to watch the opportunities start to pour in." Surely enough, maybe within two hours of waking up, before I even made it to class, the jobs kept calling. I remember getting emotional and looking up and saying, "I get it, Lord. I now see why you didn't want my line tied up."

At the end of my final, I shook Professor Bloom's hand and thanked him for everything, at the time, not even knowing if KTLA would ever call. Just as I was heading out the classroom, he signaled me to come back. He expressed how helpful I was to him in the class—going above the call of duty as a student. He said, "Alexis, put me as your reference as you continue to apply for jobs. Tell them you were my teacher's aide—because you were." This may be a small gesture to some, but held a significant amount of weight to me, as college students are still in the process of building resumes with little to no job experience or professional references. It was in that brief interaction with Professor Bloom that God was yet again, validating my hard work was not going down in vain.

That night, I met up with my dad, so we could have a celebration dinner and break my fast. After dinner, we stopped by the gas station. I felt something in my spirit say, *"Check your email one more time."* At this point, I was already on cloud nine from hearing back from so many different employers, despite being nervous about where I was going to end up. Even with my fears, I didn't ignore that voice that spoke to my spirit.

While my dad was pumping my gas, I got an email from a news director out of Oregon, which presented me with the best opportunity for my needs at the time, a news producer job. When I got the email, my eyes grew ten times larger. I held my breath in shock, so much so that I had to remind myself to breathe! At that moment, not only was God telling me which opportunity I was supposed to take but a way for Him to honor my diligence thus far by saying, "Job well done."

Acknowledgments

Aishah Randall
Maurice Thrower
Chonté Wilson
Daeshunn DuPree
L'erin Jensen
Brianna Sumler
Curtis Belvin
Clifford Breland
Ken Carrell
Katrina Dunne
Kimberly Taylor
DeMira Pierre
Alan Bloom
Solomon Kirven
Pamela Ogden
Timothy "Teach" Jones
Kevin John
Yolanda Isles

References

Burning Glass Technologies and Strada Institute for the Future of Work (2018), "The Permanent Detour: Underemployment's Long-Term Effects on the Careers of College Grads"

Depape, A.-M. R., Hakim-Larson, J., Voelker, S., Page, S., & Jackson, D. L. (2006). Self-talk and emotional intelligence in university students. *Canadian Journal of Behavioural Science / Revue canadienne des sciences du comportement, 38*(3), 250–260. https://doi.org/10.1037/cjbs2006012

"Job Offers for Class of 2019 Grads Impacted by Internship Experience." NACE. Accessed May 11, 2020. https://www.naceweb.org/job-market/trends-and-predictions/job-offers-for-class-of-2019-grads-impacted-by-internship-experience/.

Niemiec, Christopher P., and Richard M. Ryan. "Autonomy, Competence, and Relatedness in the Classroom." *Theory and Research in Education* 7, no. 2 (2009): 133–44. https://doi.org/10.1177/1477878509104318.

Nova, Annie. "Why Your First Job out of College Really, Really Matters." CNBC. CNBC, July 2, 2018. https://www.cnbc.com/2018/06/25/why-your-first-job-out-of-college-really-really-matters.html.

Plumer, Brad. "Only 27 Percent of College Grads Have a Job Related to Their Major." The Washington Post. WP Company, May 20, 2013. https://www.washingtonpost.com/news/wonk/wp/2013/05/20/only-27-percent-of-college-grads-have-a-job-related-to-their-major/.

Pirolli, Peter & Card, Stuart. (1999). Information Foraging. Psychological Review. 106. 643-675. 10.1037/0033-295X.106.4.643.

Stanley, Charles F. *Life Principles for the Graduate: Nine Truths for Living God's Way*. Nashville, TN: Thomas Nelson, 2009.

Trippett, Kesha. "God Rewards Diligence." Daughters of the King Daily Devotional , September 30, 2019. https://dot-k.com/devotions/god-rewards-diligence/.

CPSIA information can be obtained
at www.ICGtesting.com
Printed in the USA
BVHW051330300123
657301BV00012B/1064

9 781636 612379